WILLIAM D. BROWNING AND CATHERINE O. RYAN

NATURE INSIDE

A BIOPHILIC DESIGN GUIDE

RIBA Publishing

Published by RIBA Publishing, 66 Portland Place, London, W1B 1AD

ISBN 978-1-85946-903-3

Reprinted 2021 (twice)

British Library Cataloguing-in-Publication Data
A catalogue record for this book is available from the British Library.

Commissioning Editor: Elizabeth Webster
Production: Sarah-Louise Deazley
Cover: Sara Miranda Icaza
Designed and typeset: Sara Miranda Icaza
Printed and bound by Short Run Press Limited, Exeter
Cover images by Sosolimited, Daniel Aubry and Oliver Heath Design (left to right).

www.ribapublishing.com

CONTENTS

FOREWORD

BY THOMAS HEATHERWICK

FIGURE 0 HEATHERWICK STUDIO, ZEITZ MOCAA, CAPE TOWN, SOUTH AFRICA, 2017. To repurpose a decommissioned grading tower and silos as the Museum of Contemporary African Art (MOCAA), cutbacks to the concrete silos resulted in an awe-inspiring biomorphic form for the central atrium. On the upper levels of the tower, fractal window patterns impact perceptions of time and movement, reflecting a diurnal kaleidoscope of textures and colours – a highly biophilic experience without the presence of living vegetation.

'Biophilia' is a weird word. I had noticed it being used, but had got away with ignoring it – until one day one of my studio's collaborators wrote it into the brief for a project.

Initially, I had assumed that biophilia was just a pretentious and over-complicated way to express the simple and obvious point that plants are generally pretty good. But when I started properly looking into it, I learnt that this word is about much more than this – it delves deeper into ourselves and the science of our emotional responses to the world. I was fascinated, while simultaneously being embarrassed at myself for having previously dismissed it.

One of the reasons I originally set up my studio to design buildings and spaces was that I had felt that the emotional impact of new buildings in cities was being comprehensively overlooked, in favour of the cerebral, conceptual and mundane. The new buildings I was seeing, made from glass, metal and concrete, were technically amazing – bigger, taller and shinier than anything in history. But how did they make us feel? What did they do for us emotionally? The neglect of this dimension seemed to urgently need addressing.

As my own studio's projects grew from objects to buildings to entire pieces of city, I had found myself instinctively looking to nature and its lessons to create a counterpoint to the hard, monotonous environment that I had experienced around me growing up in 1970s London. These large new boxes that surrounded me as a child were frequently devoid, not just of greenery and nature, but of anything that might make me feel connected, curious or interested in what happened inside them.

As a counterpoint to the boring-ness, my team and I started gravitating towards the use of more natural materials that age and patinate over time – and the use of plants, trees and organic forms – as a way to create places that felt softer, kinder and more human in scale. We weren't sure of any science, but we were sure that the integration of a more natural approach to place-making created places that gave people a feeling of more balance and harmony.

In an age where mental health and well-being are becoming widespread problems that many of us encounter in our lives, it is now clearer than ever that, to design better buildings, society needs to reconnect with its own instinctive and emotional sensibilities. And nature can be an amazing teacher.

For the last century, the practice of architecture has been dominated by the cerebral, academic and theoretical, without a sufficient balancing factor of instinctive and emotionally intelligent thinking about how structures and spaces make us feel. Biophilia, for me, is one potential form of antidote. It's interesting because it is much broader than just being about the love of plants or the obvious benefits of greenery (Figure 0.0). It touches every aspect of design: whether we can see the sky change from within a room, or how we perceive sounds and movement, like the twitch of leaves or gentle noises of moving water. In our studio, we have become passionate about making places that people can feel an emotional connection with. We're clearer than ever that nature provides many of the clues to creating places that can be more alive.

Nature has infinite lessons for designers. Water and grasses can give a place vitality and the movement of a garden can provide a poetic contrast to the rigidity of a building. I'm equally fascinated by imperfection – by the ever-so-slight differences that give authenticity to texture; wood that shows its grain; materials that can be repaired and mature as they age. Nature has rhythms and patterns; it is complex and beautiful and always interesting. Why must everything be perfectly smooth and aligned? What's wrong with rough, raw and real?

A book dedicated to exploring biophilic design is something to celebrate and I'm delighted to be able to contribute. There is a growing body of evidence to support a way of working I had thought was simply intuitive – and principles that can now be advocated for more objectively. To create meaningful places that will endure, designers need to consider their emotional response to place, which goes beyond the old-fashioned conception of rational, linear thinking. The concept of biophilia is a brilliant way to frame a set of issues that I believe are critical to the design of the environments around us – where nature is not just a prop to achieve another aim – but instead, the overall objective should be a more natural world.

WHAT IS BIOPHILIA AND WHAT DOES IT MEAN FOR BUILDINGS AND SPACES?

FIGURE 0.1 SAVANNAH LANDSCAPE, SERENGETI, TANZANIA. With a prospect view across a sloping landscape, a tree canopy for refuge from the sun, and sometimes a water body and evidence human habitation, the savannah landscape is the quintessential biophilic environment.

'An underlying premise of incorporating nature into the built environment is that "when people are regularly in contact with nature, personal health and wellbeing will improve in a manner and to a degree that contributes meaningfully to public health, community resilience and environmental stewardship". [1]

This innate biological connection between people and nature is referred to as 'biophilia'. In 1964, the social psychologist Erich Fromm coined the term biophilia, from *bio–* (life) and *–philia* (to love), in his essay entitled 'The Heart of Man: Its Genius for Good and Evil'.[2] As an inchoate theory, biophilia began gaining traction after the 1984 publication of the eponymous title by Harvard biologist Edward O. Wilson. In *'Biophilia: The Human Bond with Other Species'*, Wilson explored experiences of nature and how they impacted his life and thinking.[3] He also came to define biophilia as 'the urge to affiliate with other forms of life'. With greater socialisation and application to the built environment, the concept has evolved to denote mankind's innate biological connection with and responsiveness to experiences of nature, both living and abiotic, as well as ephemeral and temporal.

The English landscape geographer Jay Appleton questioned what determines a preferred landscape by querying why one view is perceived as being pleasurable, or 'preferred', while another view is not.[4] Appleton parsed the preferred view into different objects and spatial qualities, identifying two key conditions: prospect, an unimpeded view through space, and refuge, a place where one's back is protected and there is some canopy overhead.

In the 'savannahh hypothesis', the concept of a preferred landscape was further elaborated upon by environmental psychologist Judith Heerwagen and biologist Gordon Orians. They posited that because the palaeontological evidence indicates that our species emerged on the African savannahhs (Figure 0.1), it is logical that we would prefer environments that replicate those conditions.[5] These environmental conditions included distant views (i.e. prospect), water, copses of shade trees (i.e. refuge from environmental conditions) and grazing animals.

In a global study of what would be a preferred piece of art, highly abstract art is the least preferred; people more often choose a landscape with a distant view down a slope, water, copses of shade trees, calm, grazing animals and some sign of human habitation.[67] The English Landscape tradition, particularly seen in the designs and Red Books of Humphry Repton, is a great example of human-created savannahhs. We replicate savannahhs in our suburban lawns, golf courses, parks and many agricultural landscapes.

A PATTERN LANGUAGE

Gathering together many different pieces of research it becomes apparent that experiences of nature in the built environment can fall into three broad categories, 'Nature in the Space', 'Natural Analogues' and 'Nature of the Space',[8] which give structure to a pattern language for biophilic design (Figure 0.2). As discrete design parameters, the patterns support the dissemination and conceptualisation of biophilic experiences in the built environment.[9]

Nature in the Space patterns (Figures 0.2.1–7) are direct experiences of nature within the built environment. Some examples of these include a view out of a window, a terrarium, the smell of potted herbs, a breeze through a room, a cool slab of marble, an aquarium, and the dappled light coming through moving leaves.

Natural Analogues (Figures 0.2.8–10) are indirect or representational experiences of nature in the built environment. Some examples of these could include floral patterns on pillows, the volute on a column, an abstracted moss as a carpet pattern, textured wood on a door handle, fossil-rich stone in a wall, and a fractal pattern in flooring.

Nature of the Space patterns (Figures 0.2.11–15) are four-dimensional characteristics of common spatial experiences in nature. In the built environment, these could include a window at the end of a corridor, a high-backed booth in a restaurant, peekaboo cut-outs in a partition, the meeting room cantilevered into the atrium and the transition from a low entry into a high-ceilinged lobby.

FIGURE 0.2 15 PATTERNS OF BIOPHILIC DESIGN.

15 PATTERNS OF BIOPHILIC DESIGN

NATURE IN THE SPACE

1. **Visual Connection with Nature** — a view to an element of nature, living systems and natural processes.

2. **Non–Visual Connection with Nature** — auditory, haptic, olfactory or other stimuli that engender a deliberate and positive reference to nature, living systems and/or natural processes.

3. **Non–Rhythmic Sensory Stimuli** — stochastic and ephemeral connection with nature that may be analysed statistically but may not be predicted precisely.

4. **Thermal and Airflow Variability** — changes in air temperature, relative humidity, airflow and/or surface temperatures that mimic natural environments.

5. **Presence of Water** — a condition that enhances the experience of a place through seeing, hearing or touching water.

6. **Dynamic and Diffuse Light** — varying intensities and colour of light and shadow that change over time to create conditions similar to those that occur in nature.

7. **Connection with Natural Systems** — awareness of natural processes, especially seasonal and temporal changes characteristic of healthy ecosystems.

NATURAL ANALOGUES

8. **Biomorphic Forms and Patterns** — symbolic references to contoured, patterned, textured or numerical arrangements that persist in nature.

9. **Material Connection with Nature** — materials and elements from nature that, through minimal processing, reflect the local ecology or geology and create a distinct sense of place.

10. **Complexity and Order** — rich sensory information that adheres to spatial hierarchies similar to those encountered in nature.

NATURE OF THE SPACE

11. **Prospect** — an unimpeded view over a distance for surveillance and decision making.

12. **Refuge** — a place for withdrawal, from environmental conditions or the main flow of activity, in which the individual is protected from behind and overhead.

13. **Mystery** — the promise of more information, achieved through partially obscured views or other sensory devices that entice the individual to venture deeper into the physical environment.

14. **Risk/Peril** — an identifiable threat coupled with a reliable safeguard.

15. **Awe** — stimuli including other biophilic patterns that defy an existing frame of reference and lead to a change in perception.

FIGURE 0.3 BIOPHILIC INTERIORS THROUGH HISTORY. (a) Moorish Islamic Great Mosque, Mezquita de Córdoba (785–987) in Córdoba, Spain; (b) Chinese ceiling of Hall of Prayers for Good Harvests at Temple of Heaven (1420) in Beijing; (c) Gothic Revival fan–vaulted ceiling of the Long Gallery at Strawberry Hill (1763) in Twickenham, London; (d) Art Nouveau entrance hall of Casa Mila (La Pedrera, 1910) on Passeig de Gracia in Barcelona, Spain; (e) Art Deco lobby lift at Swiss Center, Goelet Building (1932) in New York City; and (f) Postmodern MSP Building (2004) window seat nook, Scottish Parliament, Edinburgh.

A BRIEF HISTORY OF BIOPHILIC ARCHITECTURE

In the 12,000 years since humans began transforming the natural landscape, only in the last 250 years have modern cities become our habitat. Today, with more people living in cities than in the countryside, the built environment is an inescapable reality of everyday life. Much of our modern habitat is unnecessarily devoid of any profound connection with nature. With the trend continuing towards increased urbanisation and widespread mental and physical burnout, the need for a generous architecture that (re)connects people to an experience of nature becomes ever more important.[10]

Biophilic design research is believed by some to wisely, although merely, corroborate 'the intuitively obvious'.[11] Biophilic design transcends aesthetics and is thus represented in many architectural styles and movements throughout history (Figure 0.3); most notably from Gothic, Moorish and Islamic, to Rococo and Beaux–Arts, Japanese and Chinese, Modern and Art Deco, to Vernacular, and to Network Specifism, a twenty–first century adaptation of Critical Regionalism for 'mediating between the genius loci and the global zeitgeist'.[12]

The prevailing attitude is that while public demand for healthy buildings and nature–rich urban experiences goes a long way towards broadening adoption, design professionals and researchers are best positioned to embrace the principles of biophilic design and actively restore the human–nature connection through architecture, design and education. As this manuscript was finalised in the early months of the COVID–19 pandemic, the surge of interest in connecting with nature has been in the limelight during an unprecedented global lockdown. This book aims to translate that instinctive yearning for nature into a paradigm shift in design thinking — one that embraces biophilic architecture and design as a philosophy for enriching our communities with a healthier, convivial future.

FIGURE 0.4 ATELIER DREISEITL WITH GREENWORKS, TANNER SPRINGS PARK, PORTLAND, OR USA, 2010. Biophilic design implementation has extended from interiors to urban planning and parks. This 1-acre park features a variety of prospect and refuge conditions, while a mix of active and passive spaces offer a variety of experiences with nature and the community.

GUIDE TO USING THIS BOOK

In this book, chapters 1 and 2 outline the economic and scientific case for biophilic design; chapter 3 takes a look at art, craftsmanship, ornamentation and other aspects of biophilic design at the product scale; and chapters 4 to 12, organised by building typology, highlight unique opportunities and limitations of that particular typology or sector. Case studies in each chapter touch on perspectives, challenges and lessons learned by project teams or owners when incorporating biophilic design, while the image captions speak more directly to the patterns and design characteristics that make the space biophilic.

Case studies were selected based on the unique perspective represented, the timelessness of a biophilic solution or some other aspect of biophilia in the design process. Therefore, the projects represent a broad range of age, familiarity and scale. Some were approached with a focused intent to use biophilic design, while others exhibit a biophilic experience that evolved intuitively from the designer. Broad geographical representation was also intended, but access to quality photographs and narratives in the time period in which this manuscript was crafted did limit the breadth of potential projects. For instance, Africa and South America are largely unrepresented, despite being hotspots for Vernacular architecture and biomorphic patterning.

Some readers may gravitate towards certain chapters, while others may find useful lessons from disparate chapters or individual project examples throughout the book — an approach to biophilic design discussed in the community or residential chapters may present valuable insights for designers working on a retail or hotel project. The book concludes with closing thoughts from the authors and a 'toolkit' of resources for practitioners and students for communicating, developing and implementing biophilic design.

CHAPTER 1

THE SCIENTIFIC AND BUSINESS CASE FOR BIOPHILIC DESIGN

FIGURE 1.1 LAN SU CHINESE GARDEN, PORTLAND, OREGON, USA, 2000. A view to nature stimulates a particularly strong response in the visual cortex of the brain.

Biophilia is not a single instinct but a complex of learning rules that can be teased apart and analyzed individually. The feelings molded by the learning rules fall along several emotional spectra: from attraction to aversion, from awe to indifference, from peacefulness to fear-driven anxiety.[1]

Intuition tells us that being in nature makes us happier. However, the intuitively obvious usually needs scientific and financial evidence to convince clients to make the investment in biophilic design.

SCIENCE CASE

HEALING AND STRESS REDUCTION

American professor Roger Ulrich led one of the earliest and best known studies into health-related outcomes and biophilia.[2] Patients recovering from gall bladder surgery were placed in rooms along one side of a building. Half of the rooms had a view to a brick wall; the others had a view to some trees and shrubs. The patients were matched by demographics and paint colour of the room, with the view as the remaining variable. The patients with the view to the brick wall took an average of 8.7 days to recover, while the patients with a view to the trees took an average of 7.9 days. The patients with a view to the trees had far fewer nursing calls and took fewer painkillers. This study is one of the first examples of evidence-based design and helped to launch the healing garden movement in hospital design.

In subsequent studies with cardiac patients in Sweden, Ulrich and his team showed patients either images of nature or blank sheets of paper, before or after heart surgery. They found that patients who viewed the nature images pre- or post-surgery had lower blood pressure, lower heart rate and improved recovery times than patients who viewed the blank sheets of paper.[3]

In a similar study,[4] psychologist Peter Kahn and colleagues found that a video screen showing images of nature would lower blood pressure, lower heart rate and have positive psychological benefits for workers in a windowless space. This led Kahn to ask whether seeing simulated nature was equivalent to seeing real nature. In a study at the University of Washington,[5] participants were given a stressor, and then during the recovery task had one of three views: a wall of plain curtains; the same wall with a portion of the curtains open to reveal a view out of a window to a fountain, flowers and trees; or portions of the curtains open to reveal a high-definition flat screen television of the same dimensions and aspect ratio as the window showing in real time the view out of the window. While the view of just the curtains was not particularly helpful to the recovery process, the view out of the window and the view of the flat screen elicited similar positive psychological responses. The view shown on the flat screen television lowered blood pressure and heart rate, but not as much as the view out of the real window. Optical scientist Alan Lewis, in a 2012 personal discussion with the authors, believes that this difference in response is due to parallax from binocular vision of spatial experiences. When viewing a scene in real space, moving the head just a few millimetres changes the view, as the overlap of images from the two eyes changes. Even the best high-definition flat screen televisions cannot yet replicate parallax — the image is the same from every viewing angle.

How the brain processes experiences of nature is quite interesting. As images trigger responses in the rods and cones on the retina of the human eye, they are transmitted by the optical nerve to the visual cortex of the brain. This funnel-shaped portion of the brain does the initial processing before the images move to different parts of the brain for interpretation. As an image travels further into the funnel the cross-section of the visual cortex increases and more neurons are triggered, in particular mu opioid receptors, which leads to a more pleasurable response. Irving Biederman and Edward Vessel investigated how images of varying complexity within the built environment were processed in the visual cortex. More complex images travelled further into the funnel-shaped cortex. In the Biederman-Vessel study,[6] an image of a plain grey wall was processed at the start of the funnel, while images of a pile of bricks and a lamp post beside a building were each processed further into the cortex. Finally, an image of a rolling Japanese garden with water made it furthest into the cortex, triggering the strongest pleasure response of all

FIGURE 1.2 BARON KARL VON HASENAUER AND GOTTFRIED SEMPER, KUNSTHISTORISCHES MUSEUM, VIENNA, AUSTRIA, 1891. Ornamentation with a moderate degree of complexity can capture gaze attention and interest.

(Figure 1.1). The Japanese garden was also the only one of these images that did not elicit rapidly diminishing responses upon repeat viewing.

Using gaze attention tracking devices, it is possible to determine which elements of an view or location most capture our interest. Because of the relatively small area of vision that can be processed by the brain, the eyes dart around to produce a larger image, fixating briefly on some things and moving across others. A human face will get our attention first, typically followed by other living things. In the built environment, after person or animal, decorative detailing will attract our attention more than a blank wall (Figure 1.2).[7] This indicates that ornamentation in architecture may make for more interesting design, and in traditional design that ornamentation would frequently be derived from nature.

The brain subconsciously sorts between living and human-made or mechanical motion. Work by neuroscientist Michael Beauchamp and others[8] found that videos of a hand saw moving back and forth were processed in a part of the brain that deals with non-living objects while videos of a person moving back and forth in a similar motion as the hand saw were processed in a part of the brain that is associated with living things. Acknowledging that participants are undoubtedly aware that a saw is not alive and a moving person is alive, the experiment was repeated using videos of only motion capture dots on the saw and the person. Without knowing which object generated the motion, the brain processed the correct motions into areas dealing with either living or non-living. Non-living motion, like a pendulum, is repetitive, predictable and easily disregarded; whereas, living motion is less so, and thus more effective at capturing attention and offering visual respite.

While vision is the primary sense for most humans, and accounts for much of the brain's sensory capacity, we also experience nature through scent, sound, touch, taste, temperature, pressure, balance, distance and more.

The context or combination of senses can determine how some experiences are interpreted. For example, there are times when the sound frequency of highway traffic is very similar to that of waves on a beach. In a study of comparison, a new sound was generated by averaging the two sounds, and then played while showing either an image of waves on a beach or a highway filled with traffic. While the sound was the same, where it was processed in the brain depended on the image. Although the same sound was heard the outcomes differed: when heard with the beach image as context, the sound was processed in the part of the brain that tends to deal with living things and was reported as being a positive experience. When heard with the highway image as context, the sound was both processed in the part of the brain that tends to deal with human–made things and reported as being a neutral or negative experience.[9]

In Japan and Korea, research has been conducted to gauge the effect of walking or sitting in a forest as opposed to walking or sitting on an urban street. The time in the forest led to lower measurements of blood pressure, heart rate and the cortisol stress hormone. Cortisol levels also reportedly stayed lower for extended periods after the 'forest bathing' experience.[10][11] Many of the walks occurred in Hinoki cypress plantations, where there are significant phytoncides, or essential oils, in the air. There is evidence of positive changes in the immune system response after these experiences.[12]

Research also indicates that some scents might directly influence brain stress response. Mice exposed to the smell of linalool, one of the components of the smell of lavender, experienced a calming response. The scent appeared to trigger some of the same neurons that are activated by Valium, but without the motor impairment.[13] Mice have similar neural pathways to humans. This presents another potential way in which nature can help with stress reduction.

COGNITIVE RESPONSE

Much of the research on biophilia has focused on stress reduction as measured through heart rate, blood pressure, cortisol levels and psychological response. Another thread of research has focused on the cognitive response. As far back as the 1800s there was a theory that the brain operates differently while experiencing nature.[14] It was thought that when out in nature, the brain operates on a level of 'soft fascination'. This eventually

FIGURE 1.3 COOKFOX ARCHITECTS, COOKFOX SIXTH AVENUE STUDIO, NEW YORK CITY, USA, 2014. A nature–rich view helps to restore cognitive capacity.

became the basis for attention restoration theory (ART),[15][16] which posited that portions of the prefrontal cortex quiet down while experiencing nature. After this mental pause, we have better cognitive capacity.

A recent confirmation of the ART theory came in an experiment using functional magnetic resonance imaging (fMRI) measurement to observe brain activity. After a stressor, participants viewed either an image of an asphalt rooftop, or the same image with flowers on the rooftop. Within 40 seconds of viewing the image of the rooftop with flowers, the prefrontal cortex decreased activity and subsequently the participants performed better on the recovery task (Figure 1.3).[17]

FIGURE 1.4 EXPERIENCES OF NATURE AND
CORRESPONDING BIOLOGICAL RESPONSES.
Different biophilic design patterns support
different outcomes. See the Toolkit for
complete references.

There is also evidence that the presence of nature may help the rate of cognitive development among school-age children. A study of 2593 children in Grades 2–4 in Spain's Barcelona school system found that, separate from demographics, children in schools with more tree canopy in the schoolyard had an increased rate of cognitive development over the course of a year of measurement.[18]

In reality the effects of biophilic experiences are not just stress-reducing or cognitive impacts, but frequently a combination of both. An experiment in which participants spent five minutes seated in a windowless classroom and five minutes seated in a biophilic space — with plants, a metal screen with biomorphic patterns and a view to the river outside — found significantly different outcomes. The biophilic setting led to lower blood pressure, lower galvanic skin conductance and 14% improvement in short-term memory performance.[19]

PATTERNS AND OUTCOMES

This snapshot of scientific evidence contributed to the assemblage of 15 design patterns that were described in the Introduction. It is important to understand that different elements or patterns of nature help support different health outcomes. Some are best for stress reduction, some for cognitive function, some for mood and preference, and some help with multiple outcomes (Figure 1.4). One way to filter which lessons from science to use in a project is to understand the desired outcomes and then see which pattern supports those outcomes.

BUSINESS CASE

For some clients the scientific case for biophilic design is sufficiently compelling. Others need a business case to rationalise the incorporation of biophilic design into their project. Fortunately, early evidence of direct economic benefits of biophilic design can be recounted in examples across multiple sectors and building typologies, documenting measured increase in productivity, increased retail sales, differential hotel room rates and increased property values. As with the scientific case, evidence for the business case started a couple of decades ago.

	BIOPHILIC DESIGN PATTERN	A. IMPROVED PHYSIOLOGICAL RESPONSE	B. IMPROVED COGNITIVE FUNCTIONING	C. EMOTIONS & MOOD & PREFERENCE
1.	VISUAL CONNECTION WITH NATURE	Lowered blood pressure and heart rate; Increased parasympathetic activity	Improved mental engagement/ attentiveness	Positively impacted attitude and overall happiness; Reduced future discounting; Heightened Appreciation for Nature; Decreased Rumination; Correlation between view preference and motivation
2.	NON–VISUAL CONNECTION TO NATURE	Reduced systolic blood pressure and stress hormones; Improved Immune Function	Positively impacted cognitive performance; Improved Creativity	Perceived improvements in mental health, tranquility, and pain management; Observed Preference
3.	NON–RHYTHMIC SENSORY STIMULI	Positively impacted heart rate, systolic blood pressure and sympathetic nervous system activity		Increase dwell time and observed behavioral measures of attention and exploration
4.	THERMAL & AIRFLOW VARIABILITY	Positively impacted comfort, well–being and productivity; Fewer self–reported Sick Building Syndrome cases	Improved task performance	Improved perception of temporal and spatial pleasure (alliesthesia)
5.	PRESENCE OF WATER	Reduced stress, increased feelings of tranquility, lower heart rate and blood pressure	Positively impacted cognitive performance and creativity	Observed preferences and positive emotional responses
6.	DYNAMIC & DIFFUSE LIGHT	Positively impacted circadian system functioning; Increased Visual Comfort	Improvements to cognitive and behavioral performance	Positively impacted attitude and overall happiness
7.	CONNECTION WITH NATURAL SYSTEMS	Enhanced positive health responses; Shifted perception of environment		Enhanced positive health responses; Shifted perception of environment
8.	BIOMORPHIC FORMS & PATTERNS	Improved stress recovery	Improved learning outcomes	Observed view preference
9.	MATERIAL CONNECTION WITH NATURE	Decreased diastolic blood pressure; Improved comfort; Reduced Plasma Cortisol Level; Increased Heart Rate Variability; Self–reported calming effect		Observed material preference
10.	COMPLEXITY & ORDER	Positively impacted perceptual and physiological stress responses	Brainwave response indicative of relaxation; Improved environmental navigation; Improved learning outcomes	Subjective mood and preference response
11.	PROSPECT	Reduced stress; Improved comfort and perceived safety		Reduced boredom, irritation, fatigue; Visual Preference
12.	REFUGE	Improved perception of safety		Observed visual preference
13.	MYSTERY			Observed Visual Preference; Induced strong pleasure response
14.	RISK / PERIL			Resulted in strong dopamine or pleasure responses
15.	AWE	Reduced stress related symptoms		Increased pro–social behavior; Positive impacted attitude and overall happiness

UNPRODUCTIVE
SALARIES & BENEFITS
ABSENTEEISM 1.1%
PRESENTEEISM 1.7%
2.8%

RENT
5.1%

OPERATING COSTS
UTILITIES, TAXES, INSURANCE
CLEANING. SECURITY, ETC
1.7%

PRODUCTIVE
SALARIES & BENEFITS
90.4%

FIGURE 1.5 AVERAGE ANNUAL COMMERCIAL COSTS BY SQUARE FOOT. In the US commercial sector, as with elsewhere around the world, the occupants are by far the largest annual cost to building operations. [21]

In conversations about green building the focus frequently moves to energy savings, which is a valued measure because calculations for both CO_2 emission reductions and financial returns are easily obtained. This focus on energy performance overlooks the biggest annual cost of a facility — the cost per unit area of the employees. Absenteeism is one example of these costs, and there is evidence that the level of access to daylight and nature views can translate into a reduction in sick days.[20] In the commercial workplace, employee salaries and benefits are typically 90% of the total operational cost for a company, while rent is about 9% and energy 1% (Figure 1.5).

Due to the nature of most office work today, traditional measures of units per hour productivity are rare. However, direct calculations are possible, primarily among large-volume manufacturing facilities and call centres where very good data is recorded. As a case in point, in an experiment at the Sacramento Municipal Utility District building in California, the call centre is on an upper floor with trees outside the perimeter windows. The building has a LEED Gold certification with good indoor air quality, individual thermal controls and good daylighting. The workstations were perpendicular to the windows, so while employees were facing their computer screens, they did not have a direct view out of the window. In the experiment, workstations were rotated 11 degrees off perpendicular at a cost of US$1,000 per workstation. This repositioning allowed any outdoor movement from the trees or sky to be within the zone of peripheral vision. As the human brain is highly perceptive to movement in the peripheral vision, ephemeral experiences of leaves, birds, butterflies, rain and passing clouds capture the attention of workers at their desks. By looking outside and beyond the computer screen, the muscles in the eye relax as the lens flattens to refocus on views at greater distances. By looking out at nature for 40 seconds or more,[22] the brain has an opportunity to shift into attention restoration mode. The end result was that call handling per hour increased by over 6%, which amounted to a return on investment of US$2,999 (£2,263 in 2003) per workstation.[23][24]

In retail there are several threads of evidence for the economic basis. Bringing daylight into retail can increase sales per unit area, as evidenced in store prototypes built for Walmart and Stop&Shop.[25] On a shopping street, an increase in the number of street trees can result in higher sales for stores fronting onto that street.[26] An experiment that involved placing an aquarium in a display window in an indoor shopping mall resulted in an increase in the amount of time shoppers stopped to look at the display by 16%; the portion of shoppers who stopped also increased from 3.3% to 8.5%.[27]

Residential prices frequently reflect biophilic attributes, particularly related to access to views. In Seattle, homes on a hillside with partial lake views were 30% more valuable than those with no view, while homes with full views were 58% more valuable and lakeside homes 127% more valuable.[28]

FIGURE 1.6 CONCRETE ARCHITECTURAL ASSOCIATES, CITIZENM, TIMES SQUARE, NEW YORK CITY, USA, 2014. Lobbies with strong biophilic design have more active and passive users.

Similarly, resort hotel guest rooms with a view to water are typically priced 18% more per night than rooms with no view. In urban business hotels, rooms with a water view or view of a famous building are priced about 12% more, and rooms with a garden view are priced about 2% more. On the hotel interior, an observational study of lobbies with or without biophilic design measures found a 36% increase in the number of people who were active or passive users of the biophilic lobbies (Figure 1.6).[29] This represents a significant opportunity for hoteliers to increase revenue through food and beverage sales in the lobbies, and a strong incentive to implement biophilic design.

Looking back at to the original Ulrich study, biophilic hospital experiences supported a shortened recovery period for patients by an average of 8.5%.[30] The typical post–surgery hospital stay in the USA is 4.8 days[31] at a cost of US$4,221 per day,[32] across the 5,795 registered hospitals in the USA, which would have amounted to aggregate annual savings of more than US$89 million (£72 million).[33] The healing gardens movement in hospitals has also reportedly lowered stress levels among hospital staff,[34] with some evidence in lower turnover rates.[35]

In education, there was an unfortunate period from the late 1960s into the 1970s when many classrooms were built without windows, to limit student distractions from views to the outside. This has proven to be detrimental to learning outcomes. Much of the research on learning outcomes has focused on improvements to test scores, ranging from 7% to 18%, as a result of bringing daylight into classrooms.[36][37] Students in classrooms with a view to nature reportedly have a 13% increase in attention span compared to students in classrooms without windows or with views only to other buildings.[38]

The scientific and business case evidence helps support the increasing interest in biophilic design. For designers the critical task is to translate that evidence into effective design. Distributing a few plants around a room may help liven it up, but it's not necessarily the most effective way to elicit a positive cognitive, physiological and psychological response. A clear, intentional process helps to optimise the impact of biophilic design in any space and on any type of project, from interiors to campus scale.

CHAPTER 2

BIOPHILIA IN THE DESIGN PROCESS

FIGURE 2.1 KENGO KUMA AND ASSOCIATES, THE FOREST, VALEXTRA, MILAN, ITALY, 2018. With the goal of creating 'a sense of romantic escapism', the design team utilised perceptions of mystery to both draw attention to individual products and entice visitors to 'roam among them as if walking in a forest'. Raw wood planks offer texture and scent for a timeless, multisensory retail experience.

FIGURE 2.2 ART AQUA, BIETIGHEIM–BISSINGEN, GERMANY, 2014. The offices of German green wall and water wall manufacturer art aqua GmbH & Co. serve as both testing laboratory and showroom for their products, offering potential clients the opportunity to experience different types of green walls and water walls in an active, open–plan workplace setting.

Biophilic design is a philosophy that implores practitioners to draw correlations between nature, the built environment, the human experience and design decisions. While a biophilic design strategy is conceivably replicable, the inspiration, activities and resulting design solutions will expectedly vary in accordance with architectural processes, the characteristics unique to each project and site, and the priorities of the people engaged to make it all happen.

While biophilic design is sometimes intuitive, integrative design planning and management helps to ensure the team priorities remain aligned and the vision for health and well–being oriented experience is met (Figure 2.1). How well the biophilic design opportunity is principled, contextualised, integrated, managed and documented in the architectural process will influence the long–term efficacy for a project.

This chapter presents a brief compendium of perspectives and activities, rather than a step–by–step guide, for incorporating biophilic design into projects with experiential health and wellness preferences or goals. See the Toolkit for additional resources and worksheets for project teams to talk through ideas and actively contribute to a biophilic design agenda.

PRINCIPLES OF BIOPHILIC DESIGN

Principles of biophilic design are 'fundamental conditions for the effective practice of biophilic design',[1] communicating a vision of health and well-being in symbiosis with nature. The principles support an adaptable methodology for realising that vision.

1. Biophilic design requires repeated and sustained engagement with nature.
2. Biophilic design focuses on human adaptations to the natural world that over evolutionary time have advanced people's health, fitness and well-being.
3. Biophilic design encourages an emotional attachment to particular settings and places.

4. Biophilic design promotes positive interactions between people and nature that encourage an expanded sense of relationship and responsibility for human and natural communities.
5. Biophilic design encourages mutually reinforcing, interconnected and integrative architectural solutions.

The five principles of biophilic design transcend architectural design aesthetics, serving as yardsticks for success. These principles are universal — benefitting a majority of people and places — and are the forerunners to the characterisation of the more familiar nature–inspired strategies and patterns that yield meaningful biophilic experiences.

CONTEXTUALISING THE OPPORTUNITY

As a process of discovery, context originates from multiple sources, most evidently from site characteristics, desired experiential outcomes and value proposition.

SITE CONTEXT

Ecology of place, the existing built environment and the community are three primary sources of site context — much like background research that is conducted for any architectural design or master planning project, but through the lens of biophilia. Ecology of place considers the local climate, geography and habitat to inform everything from fenestration to plant species selection. The existing built environment context considers a structure's spatial conditions, local architectural vernacular and adjacent physical neighbourhood. Community context considers the local industry, stakeholder groups, cultures and traditions of the local people and place and how they can each inspire and guide new design concepts. Thus, much like how an interior design motif based on the colour palette of the diverse and rugged American Northwest would differ from that of Thailand's tropical coast along the Andaman Sea, the palette of biophilic design patterns may vary for projects in each of these locations and would likely result in different design solutions (Figure 2.3).

FIGURE 2.3A The wood construction and natural ventilation of the Amanpuri in Phuket, Thailand, reference a vernacular architecture, while the positioning of this resort living room, up on a cliff overlooking the Andaman Sea, is an adaptation to the land contours and climate.

FIGURE 2.3B The lobby living room of the Kimpton Monaco Hotel in Portland, Oregon, USA, is reflective of a melding of cultures — bright colours are a great response to a cold and overcast climate, while the bedrooms are distinctly influenced by the earthen colours of the local terrain and wildlife.

TABLE. 2.1 Contextual drivers for prioritising biophilic design patterns.

Identifying what is 'free' on site — existing physical, natural and cultural site characteristics (Table. 2.1) — can help clarify feasibility in efficiently and effectively celebrating and working with the site context.

Contextualisation is an ongoing process that can occur during site selection and feasibility, when conducting site studies (e.g. daylight, biodiversity, solar and wind capacity), as part of the background research into site history and during the design iteration process. As there are countless potential biophilic design solutions, upholding context as a driver for design decisions helps to continuously refine a biophilic design strategy.

EXPERIENTIAL CONTEXT

Assumptions about experiential needs can be made based on the type of facility, i.e. school, residence, office, civic, healthcare, light manufacturing. Having a general sense of the client goals and values, site programme, occupant type and occupant activities helps to identify more targeted experiential goals for the project (Table 2.2). Organisational dynamics — whether departmentalised, collaborative, relational or transactional — indicate a relative spectrum of potential biophilic experiences (e.g. ratio of open–plan to refuge spaces), as do the nuances of user sub–groups that may depend upon different methods or styles of learning, working or healing. Exploring experiential needs and wants helps to narrow down when and where in the design process biophilic design interventions are incorporated.

VALUE PROPOSITION

The value of any biophilic design solution is inherently linked to its intended experience. While return on investment is a common determinant of buy–in, the intrinsic value of a biophilic solution is often more complex than the investment cost alone. The value proposition increases as the breadth of impact expands from one outcome to many. Outcomes may encompass occupant experience, employee satisfaction, measurable health benefits (e.g. reduction in absenteeism and health claims), greater social cohesion, pricing and purchasing behaviours, stronger brand identity or market differentiation — all measurements realised well after initial investment.

PATTERN PRIORITISATION FILTERS	CHARACTERISTICS AND METRICS
Desired health and well-being outcomes	creativity, analytics, recovery
User type/group	activity patterns or behaviours
Space programming	needs and wants
Local climate and ecosystem	zone, habitat, cycles, diurnal patterns
Local culture or heritage	indigenous building materials and practices, textiles, experiences
Environmental goals	carbon, energy, habitat, water, waste
What is 'free' on site	access to daylight and airflow; existence of a central stair or balcony; proximity to local materials or forested park; history of building use
What is already measured	absenteeism, occupant satisfaction; green building metrics

FIGURE 24 BIOPHILIC STAIN FINISH

The most effective biophilic experiences are integral to the overall project concept. The value proposition for a given project therefore needs to be established during the concept design phase and continuously championed. Value propositions also create a framework for disseminating biophilic design priorities. Tying a desired experiential outcome, and biophilic design principle or pattern, to a value proposition is a way to continually reinforce the desired project outcome.

PLANNING FOR INTEGRATIVE DESIGN

As the efficacy of a biophilic design solution is not easily measured by a checklist or performance modelling, successful biophilic design planning depends upon alignment of desired health outcomes and experiences with design opportunities.

The following activities are examples of ways to engage biophilic design thinking in the architecture and design processes. These activities may already be familiar to designers and could thus be easily adapted to help narrow the focus for arriving at a suitable biophilic design strategy regardless of project scale or typology.

GAP ANALYSIS

Gap analysis is a review of existing conditions or proposed design plans and the potential for meeting new project goals. Projects with a biophilic design agenda can benefit from a gap analysis as a component of site selection and assessment, design planning or design plan peer review processes. A gap analysis can be as thorough or focused as desired, and is a particularly effective tool for identifying absent experiences (e.g. adequate daylight, spatial qualities that could support restoration) deemed crucial to supporting health and well-being in that particular space.

Identifying desired health outcomes (e.g. reduced symptoms of depression among patients) and associated biophilic patterns (e.g. daylight; refuge spaces) before conducting a gap analysis is not essential, but may result in a more informative and actionable analysis. For projects that do not yet have clearly established biophilic design goals, the five biophilic design principles offer a good baseline framework to start a gap analysis. A health outcomes matrix or pattern language can also be used to give structure to a gap analysis. See the Toolkit for a sample gap analysis and supporting materials.

WORKSHOPPING THE DESIGN OPPORTUNITY

The purpose of workshopping the biophilic design opportunity is to identify priorities for health and well-being, build consensus for experiential design, understand contextual constraints, set goals and inspire the team with biophilic design precedents. This convening of project stakeholders can also result in new directions for interdisciplinary collaboration.

Workshopping that includes discussions around what is already measured by the building or occupant/owner (e.g. absenteeism, health complaints) can provide insight into what is valued and how certain biophilic design solutions may also be able to enhance building performance.

Biophilic design workshops and charrettes add the greatest value and insight when held in the late concept or early schematic design phase. When time permits, a charrette dedicated to biophilic experiences or occupant health and well-being communicates it as a priority and allows the team to stay on topic for the duration of the meeting.

DESIGN NARRATIVE

A biophilic design narrative communicates the principles of biophilic design in terms of the desired human experience of a particular building or landscape.

A narrative can be used to communicate the 'why' behind design decisions, from space planning to fenestration to materials palette. Biophilic design narratives can be written statements, two-dimensional storyboards, augmented or virtual reality walkthroughs or similar. The chosen communication style, often dictated by design firm culture or client preference, is less important than the conveyance of biophilic design intent to all disciplines, not just the architect.

Circling back to the narrative periodically is a best practice for keeping the biophilic design strategies aligned with the vision and principles. The narrative may evolve over the life of the project, but ultimately serves as a guidance and reference tool for the duration of the design development process, and as a foundation for a client or community-facing narrative after occupancy.

BIOPHILIC INTENSITY MAPPING AND PATTERN PRIORITISATION

With so many ways to incorporate nature into the built environment, a deliberate effort at narrowing down which biophilic design patterns best support the project and where they are to be located is essential to creating an effective and affordable biophilic design strategy. The contextualisation of a project (i.e. site and experiential context and value proposition) is a primary resource for pattern prioritisation. The most effective biophilic design experiences emphasise a few patterns with particular thoughtfulness and rigour, applying secondary patterns as enhancements to those experiences.

A spatial overlay of stress points or desired experiences with programming can help confirm key areas for the design team to focus on in order to optimise efficacy of biophilic experiences, mitigate stress, and enhance wayfinding and signage. This is of particular value to projects with significant footprint or with highly variable programming or occupancy patterns, as not all spaces need to sustain an equal intensity of a biophilic experience. Biophilic intensity mapping assists in honing in on the areas with the greatest potential impact while curbing investment costs.

MANAGING IMPACT

Impact management for a biophilic project is the thoughtful consideration of a strategy or intervention for the right place, time and purpose, and in a way that upholds one or more of the principles of biophilic design for an acceptable duration after project completion. Impact management requires leadership commitment, as well as the ability to anticipate project schedule impacts, leverage interdisciplinary coordination opportunities, and accommodate for post–occupancy operational impact, all to ensure optimal efficiency and protect against deletion through quantity surveying (or cost engineering) or neglect.

LEADERSHIP COMMITMENT

Client and design team leadership are essential to the success and long–term persistence of the biophilic experience.

Ineffectual leadership can relegate biophilic design initiatives to fits and starts along the design process. This can lead to token interventions unable to withstand quantity surveying or cost engineering exercises, unable to sustain the desired impact after project completion, or risk being labelled as greenwashing. In this context, greenwashing is the implementation or promotion of a strategy that appears to be biophilic in design yet whose placement or orientation, relative to targeted user group(s), is grossly inadequate for achieving the intended health outcomes. A common example would be of a project with a bold green wall purportedly installed to help reduce workplace stress yet designed to be visible only from within the lobby when entering and exiting the building. While the green wall may have been a powerful marketing tactic, being unavailable to most occupants most of the day, it would have been ineffective at achieving meaningful impact to health and well–being.

A clear commitment and vision help to ensure the design process pursues a path toward authentic biophilic design. There are a variety of ways to communicate leadership commitment (Table 2.2) for biophilic design, which may vary depending on the culture of the client, design firm, project type and value proposition.

SITE SELECTION AND BIOPHILIC DESIGN FEASIBILITY

Making connections with nature can begin at any point in the timeline of a programme or project. One of the most significant opportunities is in establishing biophilic design parameters during the property identification and acquisition period.

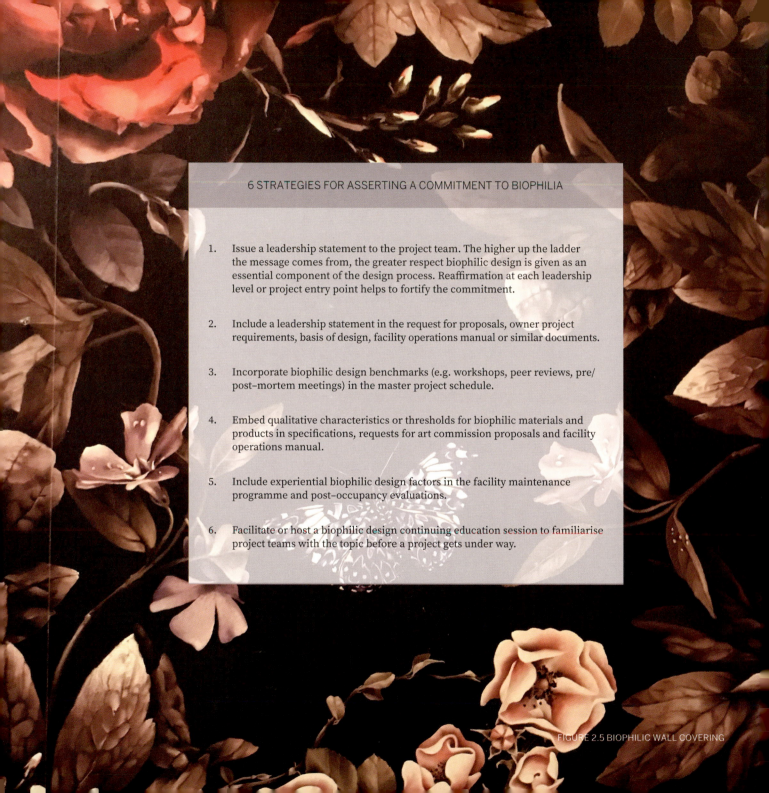

6 STRATEGIES FOR ASSERTING A COMMITMENT TO BIOPHILIA

1. Issue a leadership statement to the project team. The higher up the ladder the message comes from, the greater respect biophilic design is given as an essential component of the design process. Reaffirmation at each leadership level or project entry point helps to fortify the commitment.

2. Include a leadership statement in the request for proposals, owner project requirements, basis of design, facility operations manual or similar documents.

3. Incorporate biophilic design benchmarks (e.g. workshops, peer reviews, pre/post-mortem meetings) in the master project schedule.

4. Embed qualitative characteristics or thresholds for biophilic materials and products in specifications, requests for art commission proposals and facility operations manual.

5. Include experiential biophilic design factors in the facility maintenance programme and post-occupancy evaluations.

6. Facilitate or host a biophilic design continuing education session to familiarise project teams with the topic before a project gets under way.

FIGURE 2.5 BIOPHILIC WALL COVERING

Tasked with finding suitable properties, real estate professionals can add basic biophilic design parameters to the list of 'must–haves'. Access to daylight, views and outdoor space are among the most common nature–based parameters for property searches. Operable windows, high ceilings and shallow floorplates are also fairly common parameters.

When change feasibility is being assessed for elevations, building geometry, load capacity or other significant alterations, the viability of achieving an optimal biophilic experience can be incorporated into the assessment relative to site characteristics and projected programme.

PROJECT SCHEDULE

Once a project is under way, benchmarks and deadlines for biophilic design help to keep implementation progress on track with the rest of the architectural and interior design process. With so many potential entry points for biophilic design, recognising when in the process fundamental interventions need to occur, relative to optimisations and/or enhancements (Figure 2.6), helps with organising what can be accomplished at each phase of the project and when critical decisions need to be made. Fundamental biophilic design strategies (e.g. spatial strategies) occur at the start of the concept development to help ensure they become integral to the overall design. Optimisation of biophilic strategies (e.g. orientation, size, materiality, technical integration) and critical peer reviews occur during schematic and design development phases. Minor biophilic interventions are typically limited to supplemental strategies (e.g. accents, furniture, décor, potted vegetation) that enhance an existing strategy.

The importance of timely scheduling of biophilic design process activities and benchmarks increases on fast–tracked and design–build projects. With the growing adoption of BIM as a living document accessible to many disciplines on a project, foresight to incorporate biophilic design parameters and 'object data' into BIM execution plans and mock–ups, particularly for 3D modelling (and eventually for facilities management to maintain as–built conditions), may help to clarify building end–use goals and desired biophilic experiences to the broader design and construction team.

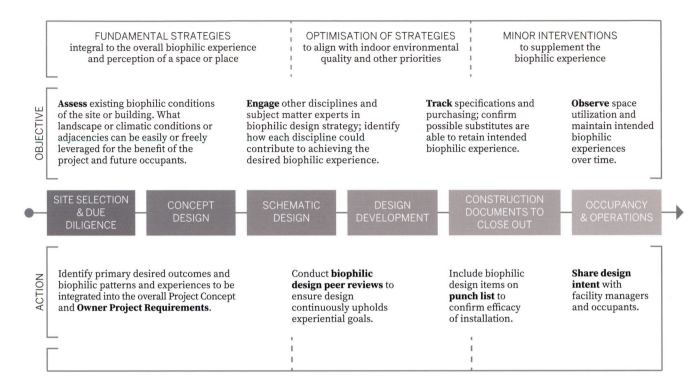

FUNDAMENTAL STRATEGIES
integral to the overall biophilic experience
and perception of a space or place

OPTIMISATION OF STRATEGIES
to align with indoor environmental
quality and other priorities

MINOR INTERVENTIONS
to supplement the
biophilic experience

OBJECTIVE

Assess existing biophilic conditions of the site or building. What landscape or climatic conditions or adjacencies can be easily or freely leveraged for the benefit of the project and future occupants.

Engage other disciplines and subject matter experts in biophilic design strategy; identify how each discipline could contribute to achieving the desired biophilic experience.

Track specifications and purchasing; confirm possible substitutes are able to retain intended biophilic experience.

Observe space utilization and maintain intended biophilic experiences over time.

| SITE SELECTION & DUE DILIGENCE | CONCEPT DESIGN | SCHEMATIC DESIGN | DESIGN DEVELOPMENT | CONSTRUCTION DOCUMENTS TO CLOSE OUT | OCCUPANCY & OPERATIONS |

ACTION

Identify primary desired outcomes and biophilic patterns and experiences to be integrated into the overall Project Concept and **Owner Project Requirements**.

Conduct **biophilic design peer reviews** to ensure design continuously upholds experiential goals.

Include biophilic design items on **punch list** to confirm efficacy of installation.

Share design intent with facility managers and occupants.

FIGURE 2.6 DECISION TIMELINE FOR BIOPHILIC DESIGN IMPLEMENTATION. The point at which biophilic design concepts are introduced on a project could significantly influence feasibility and efficacy. Yet with so many opportunities to incorporate nature and health goals, every project schedule may reflect different priorities. This schedule offers high-level objectives and actions that could be adapted for any project.

PROGRAMMING AND MICROPROGRAMMING

Accounting for the projected diversity of occupants, activities and breadth of needs is an essential aspect of biophilic design planning. Waiting until after programming is complete to introduce biophilic design concepts can be problematic. For instance, office programming tends to prioritise workspace and meeting space. Prospect views and refuge space are commonly overlooked or inadequate. A battle over workstation partition heights inevitably ensues to find a balance between privacy and prospect views. When biophilic design is part of the programming stage — when experiential requirements are discussed in parallel with functional and navigational requirements — the biophilic design perspective becomes a proactive and integral component of the overall concept rather than reactive to the final programme.

INTERDISCIPLINARY COORDINATION

Biophilic design solutions conceived of as a collaboration between the design and engineering teams and/or building facilities engineers can lead to unique, building-specific solutions with potential to yield auxiliary benefits. Integrative, multi-purpose biophilic design solutions (Figure 2.7) are also at reduced risk of being priced out of the design, or of the design being either qualitatively diminished or difficult to maintain, which can lead to a loss in efficacy too soon after first day of occupancy.

A kit-of-parts for instance (e.g. for modular designs in office workstations, school classrooms, hotel guest rooms, hospital patient rooms), necessitates close coordination of lighting, textiles, furniture and hardware to achieve a unified biophilic experience that is more likely to endure quantity surveying or cost engineering exercises. This is because the biophilic characteristics are systemic and integral — spatially, contextually, physically — to the kit-of-parts concept, rather than as individual components distributed throughout a floor plan.

Operational impact areas to consider include adaptability or controllability of biophilic design features and potential technology obsolescence. Incorporation of experiential factors (e.g. lighting colour and temperature, viewsheds, seating options) and maintenance considerations, particularly with water features or living vegetation installations, help to ensure the desired occupant experience is upheld over time.

At the end of construction, including biophilic design specifications on the punch list helps to curtail coordination oversights and ensure functionality and efficacy of final design intent before occupancy. This approach may be particularly valued on projects with highly targeted health outcomes, sensitive user groups or user expectations.

CLOSING THE FEEDBACK LOOP

Closing the feedback loop — a sharing of lessons learned from past mistakes and successes — is one of the most common lost opportunities in the practice of biophilic design. Critique both of design solutions and the process by which those solutions were conceived is essential to recognising opportunities for improved implementation, efficacy and adoption. There are several methods for supporting a healthy feedback loop and evolving biophilic design in practice. Design feedback loops (e.g. peer reviews, post-occupancy evaluations, case studies) are increasingly becoming best practices for biophilic design strategies and solutions. Implementation feedback loops (e.g. post-mortem project management assessments, some certification paths), proffering targeted assessment of the process, hold great potential for closing the feedback loop on biophilic design in the architectural process.

PEER REVIEWS

A peer review of design plans is a proactive assessment of the appropriateness and potential effectiveness of an evolving strategy and each associated biophilic design intervention. Peer reviews always link back to the prioritised biophilic design principles, outcomes, patterns and desired occupant experience. Common goals of a biophilic design peer review are to identify unforeseen design opportunities; to flag interdisciplinary oversights; to cross-check design progress with gap analyses; to curb inefficiencies in experiential impact; and to mitigate elimination through quantity surveying or cost engineering.

Biophilic design peer reviews can be facilitated at any scale of a project, from a single product or intervention to a room, building, community, town or region. Peer reviews typically take the form of either benchmarked or opportunistic design assessments, with one or more design disciplines, strategies (e.g. day-in-the-life of the occupant) or site programmes (e.g. kitchen, office, dining area, guest room, classroom, lobby, courtyard). Useful peer review materials include floor plans (see example in Figure 10.3a), architectural elevations, lighting schemes, renderings, material palettes, microprogramming layout and/or design narratives.

One review per design phase (i.e. conceptual design, schematic design, design development) is a common approach (Figure 2.6) and usually adequate for projects with small footprints. Particularly large or complex projects often benefit from additional reviews in one or more phases. In traditional phasing, peer reviews can be easily scheduled in advance of major phase benchmarks (e.g. 30% schematic design). For projects with a modified schedule, 'percentage completion' may not be the best benchmark. Setting goals early and firming up a peer review schedule are critical to design–build and fast–tracked projects as the speed at which the project is moving may inadvertently overlook biophilic design priorities.

A common practice is to squeeze in a biophilic design review shortly before a major design set deadline. The downside to this approach is that, regardless of how fruitful the discussions are perceived to be, it leaves little time or capacity for design teams to respond with meaningful revisions before the design set deadline. Facilitating a biophilic design review a few weeks in advance of a design set deadline is more likely to result in actionable recommendations. Biophilic design reviews scheduled before costing exercises and pricing sets also help to ensure accurate representation of the latest design thinking.

Peer reviews do not need to be costly or time–intensive. With clear biophilic design goals in place, a review can take between a few hours and a few days to complete (depending on the scale) and involve as few or as many people as deemed appropriate for the project phase, topic and complexity of issues.

PRE– AND POST– MORTEM ASSESSMENTS

Post–mortem assessments, although one of the most undervalued process components, are essential for improving on the implementation process and for evolving biophilic design into intuitive practice. Owners and project teams may reflect on what worked and what could have been approached differently, but documenting this feedback for use on future projects is uncommon. Knowledge often remains with the individual designers or project executive and rarely filters into the larger pool of resources that help improve and evolve the process for a design team or company.

While constructive reflection of lessons learned is often hard to implement without having a standardised protocol in place, internal assessments can happen periodically over the course of a project, such as after a biophilic design peer review or design set submission, or as a component of the close-out process. The most appropriate approach to critique will depend on the culture and dynamic of the company or team of designers. Biophilic design perspectives to assess may include success in dissemination of biophilic design priorities, scheduling and implementation of biophilic design activities, availability of subject matter expertise and interdisciplinary communication on integrative biophilic design solutions.

Post-mortem assessments can also be informed by post-occupancy evaluations, which can reveal how users are responding to the biophilic design elements. This can be done through physical measurements, surveys and biometric testing of occupants. Some techniques include eye movement tracking, cortisol sampling and heart-rate variability monitoring. The cost of biometric testing has dropped significantly in the last few years. Publishing the results of these studies helps support the further development and practice of biophilic design.

STANDARDISATION AND CERTIFICATION PATHWAYS

Environmental disciplines are rife with metrics using measurement and precedent as validation factors. As a design philosophy, biophilia does not lend itself well to quantification. Health-oriented metrics in post-occupancy evaluations can establish precedent for biophilic design choices; however, no two projects are designed and measured in the same way. Each with countless variables, precedents are rarely truly analogous but are sometimes inadvertently tools of misguidance.

As biophilic design is primarily a qualitative framework — whereby more is not necessarily better and there are endless solutions depending on the

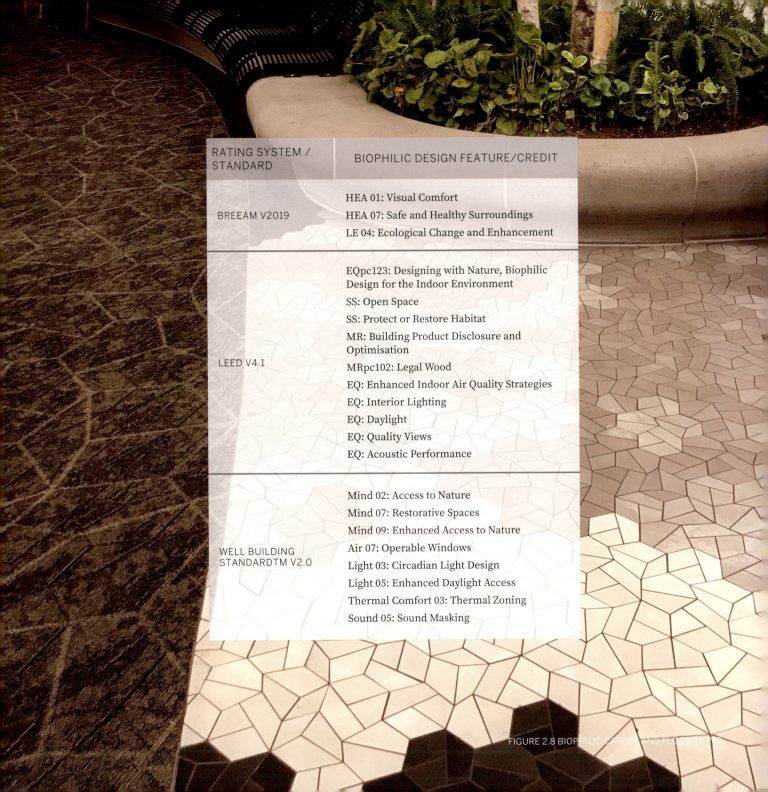

RATING SYSTEM / STANDARD	BIOPHILIC DESIGN FEATURE/CREDIT
BREEAM V2019	HEA 01: Visual Comfort HEA 07: Safe and Healthy Surroundings LE 04: Ecological Change and Enhancement
LEED V4.1	EQpc123: Designing with Nature, Biophilic Design for the Indoor Environment SS: Open Space SS: Protect or Restore Habitat MR: Building Product Disclosure and Optimisation MRpc102: Legal Wood EQ: Enhanced Indoor Air Quality Strategies EQ: Interior Lighting EQ: Daylight EQ: Quality Views EQ: Acoustic Performance
WELL BUILDING STANDARDTM V2.0	Mind 02: Access to Nature Mind 07: Restorative Spaces Mind 09: Enhanced Access to Nature Air 07: Operable Windows Light 03: Circadian Light Design Light 05: Enhanced Daylight Access Thermal Comfort 03: Thermal Zoning Sound 05: Sound Masking

FIGURE 2.8 BIOPHILIC CARPET AND FLOOR TILING

needs and priorities of people and place — performance-based certifications and point-based rating systems are not wholly condign tools for measuring design impact and efficacy. The primary advantages that standards and certifications offer are the opportunity for design teams to align biophilic design strategies with green building project performance goals within a replicable documentation framework.

Many green building standards and rating systems — BREEAM, Green Star, LEED, LBC, SITES, WELL and others — incorporate biophilic design, some more directly so than others (Figure 2.8). Synergies with each of these programmes are outlined in the Toolkit.

RECOGNITION AND AWARDS

As industry recognition is a driver of creativity and innovation, public reporting, awards and certifications each present an avenue for documenting successes and lessons learned. These pathways have the potential to further educate and inspire the design community as well as tenants and owners new to biophilic design.

The Stephen R. Kellert Biophilic Design Award,[2] established in 2017 and administered by the International Living Future Institute, is the first awards programme to recognise projects that have successfully incorporated biophilic experiences into the built environment.

CASE STUDIES AND BEST PRACTICES

Storytelling is a hallmark of expression for practitioners of biophilic design and case studies are one of the most requested resources for asserting precedence. However, with few exceptions to date, documentation of biophilic design is anecdotal, with descriptions of the design solution and perceived benefits and less on the lessons learned from decision-making processes and in situ field research.

This book introduces several case studies with the intention of drawing attention not just to great design examples but to the decisions that lead to each biophilic solution.

CHAPTER 3

INTIMATE SCALE:
BIOPHILIC ARTS AND CRAFTSMANSHIP

FIGURE 3.1 OWEN JONES, THE GRAMMAR OF ORNAMENT, 1856. Elizabethan decorations for fabrics, wood, plaster and painting by Jones, William Morris and others were intended to counteract the impact of industrialisation by reconnecting people with nature and handicraft.

FIGURE 3.2 OBSIDIAN.AGENCY FOR ROLLOUT. CA, UNDO, 2019. Dutch creative agency Obsidian used advanced software to develop a series of scalable, biophilic wallpaper designs aimed at supporting well-being and increasing focus and creativity. The perceived depth and texture of the 'Undo' product compels passers-by to edge closer and touch it.

HISTORICAL CONTEXT

Whether ostentatious or economical, architectural and interior details and décor have long been inspired by nature — from textiles and furniture, to hardware and mouldings, artwork and chinaware. For confirmation, we need only look to the arabesques and mosaics of Islamic expression, vegetal textiles and ornamentation as depicted by William Morris and Owen Jones (Figure 3.1), the decorative façade cartouche of Louis Henry Sullivan, the mastery of texture, light and shadow in traditional Japanese teahouse architecture, the beloved glassworks of Louis Comfort Tiffany and the stylised organic murals and unique ironwork of Victor Pierre Horta.

After falling out of favour in the mid-twentieth century, ornamentation and craftsmanship have benefited from an upswing in popularity in recent decades. Some patterns are particularly resilient, enduring the test of time. The nature-rich designs of William Morris have been particularly tenacious through the decades, crossing from tapestries and wall coverings, to dress shirts, notebook covers and gift-wrapping paper.

DESIGN IMPACT OPPORTUNITY

As biophilic ornamentation and patterning have persisted for thousands of years, they do not adhere to any one style or aesthetic, but rather to culture and place.

The geography, geology, ecology and climate of a place influence the human activity that gives rise to the identity of a location. Plants and wildlife, as well as agricultural, fishing and hunting practices, natural resource extraction and building materials and traditions each contribute to the inspiration for site-based biophilic design. This remains as true at the building scale as at the small scale of product design and ornamentation, where the connection between nature and the individual is more intimate.

Biophilic arts and craftsmanship proffer an enhanced sensory experience — through light, texture, density, radiant temperature and visual complexity

— in a way that is not as easily attainable or practical at a larger spatial scale. Key opportunities can be found with interior refreshes, independent art installations or as components of a comprehensive biophilic design strategy for a renovation or new-build project. Furniture and hardware, fixtures, textiles, art installations and other architectural components offer the possibility of transitioning from a visual to haptic experience. Minute design gestures can offer moments of joy and intrigue with each clutch of a door handle, finger stroke of a live-edge wooden table, or mood-shifting warmth of a flame-finished stone wall.

Not all products are created equally. At the interiors fit-out scale, the issue is not necessarily one of cost but of informed decision-making. For any project destined to have a carpet or rug, furniture, textiles, hardware or similar goods (Figure 3.2), biophilic design presents a lens and filter both for narrowing down the pool of goods and materials to select from and for coordinating a unified vision for the occupant experience. Finding the right balance of these components is essential to reaching a biophilic interior solution (Figure 3.16); the balance may be perceived as achieving 'authenticity', while avoiding tchotchkes that offer little to no experiential value or, in an extreme case, lead to visual toxicity.

See the Toolkit for more perspectives on biophilic patterning and placement.

FURNITURE

Biophilic characteristics of furniture include nature-inspired materiality and haptic experience, organic form, implied cultural ties through craftsmanship or patterning, graceful aging and patina, or a meaningful contribution to the spatial experience (Figure 3.3). It is unlikely that any single piece of furniture will embody all of these characteristics. The tactile experience of an ordinary freestanding bureau of drawers can be enhanced with biophilic pulls or handles; age, craftsmanship and a connection with nature can be expressed through wood slab table tops with coarse edges, exposed grain and bowtie joiners; and the distinct spatial experiences of prospect and refuge can be created with wingback chairs, a high-backed booth or a canopy bed.

FIGURE 3.3. BIOPHILIC FURNITURE.

FIGURE 3.4 BIOPHILIC LAMPSHADES

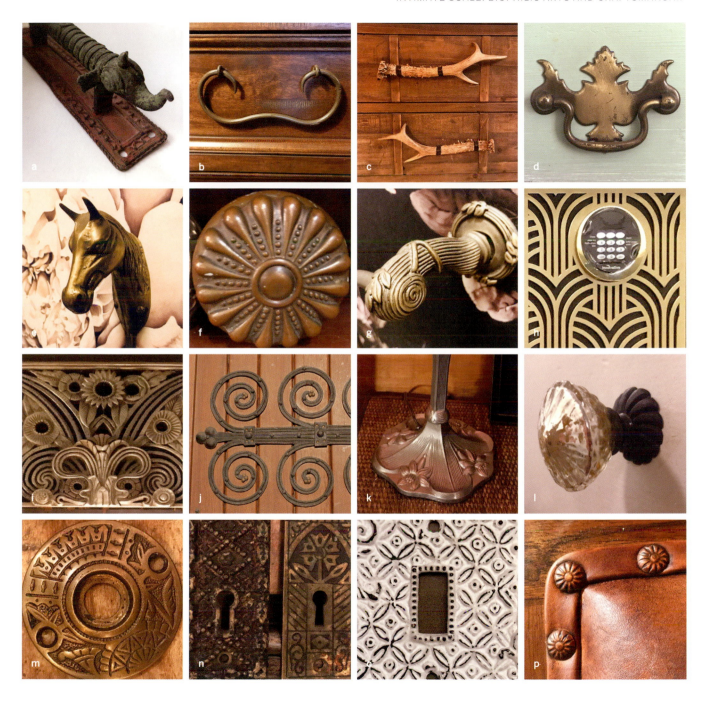

FIGURE 3.5 BIOPHILIC HARDWARE

FIXTURES

Scalloped sinks, claw-footed baths and ornate pendant lights are quintessential biophilic fixtures. Waterfall and rainfall shower head fixtures celebrate the experience of water, while lighting fixtures can be biophilic either in form (e.g. metalwork) or through the manipulation of light and colour (e.g. perforation, reflectivity) and the choice of materials or patterns (Figure 3.4). Tiffany lamps are an enduring example. Off-the-shelf lampshades with biophilic characteristics are low-hanging fruit for incorporating a nature connection.

HARDWARE

Hardware naturally offers both a haptic experience of texture, form and radiant temperature, and a visual experience of form, complexity and order, affordance and implied strength. Hinges and hooks, knobs and handles, keyhole and switch plates, vent grilles and other architectural and decorative ironworks (Figure 3.5) can each help thread a coherent vision through a biophilic design concept. Floral motifs are among the most common patterns for hardware. While selection may be driven by aesthetics and cost, hardware specifications can deliberately include parameters for tactile and visual references to nature. (See Case Study 4.4 for an owner's perspective.)

ARCHITECTURAL COMPONENTS AND MILLWORK

Column capitals, mouldings and medallions, banisters and railings, mantels, window and door frames, architectural screens and partitions, as well as permanent window treatments and other millwork, are frequently embellished with biomorphic forms and representations of nature (Figure 3.6). Perforations in screens and grilles can be designed with biomorphic forms or fractals (see Toolkit A2).

TEXTILES

Traditional textile designs from around the world make direct or indirect references to nature (Figure 3.7). Carpets, area and accent rugs, upholstery and decorative pillows, bedding, fabric window treatments and wall décor offer an array of pathways for introducing biophilic characteristics into an interior design plan. Biophilic textiles can introduce or complement visual

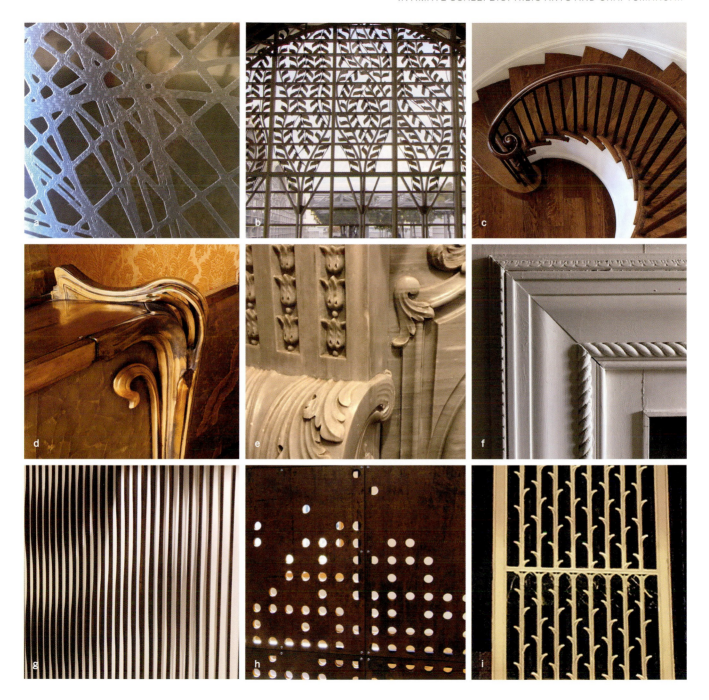

FIGURE 3.6 BIOPHILIC ARCHITECTURAL COMPONENTS AND MILLWORK

FIGURE 3.7 BIOPHILIC TEXTILES

FIGURE 3.8 BIOPHILIC FINISHES

complexity, depth and tactile variability to a materials palette and present an opportunity to explore illustrative and abstracted representations of nature. The use of repeating or statistical fractals (see Toolkit A2 and J), effective for gaining attention and reducing stress, have become a popular design strategy for companies with new lines of carpet and carpet tiles.

FINISHES

Paints and varnishes, floor and ceiling tiles, wall coverings and flooring offer multiple opportunities for biophilic content. Patterning, implied textures and representations of nature are good visual strategies, while dimensional textures, materiality and differing thermal conductance add to a multisensory experience. Examples of biophilic finishes (Figure 3.8) include wood, cork, bamboo, coarse or veined stone; washes or stains that retain evidence of wood grain; and ceramic, clay or glass tiles that play with light, colour or texture.

ART AND INSTALLATIONS

Paintings, sculptures, micro-gardens or terrariums, water features and dynamic or multifaceted installations (Figure 3.9) each present an entry point for bespoke infusions of biophilic design. Biophilic art installations can be commissioned to enhance a connection to place (through history, culture or ecology), to engender a particular feeling or experience (as sensory, temporal or ephemeral) and to impart knowledge (to entice, remind or guide). Biophilic art can be particularly effective at adding texture, dimension or cultural connectivity to a minimalist interior.

A common lost opportunity is with corridor and hallway termination points, where focusing on a piece of art or framing an outdoor view can animate an otherwise stagnant space. In large buildings, termination points are prime junctures for wayfinding interventions that can be grounded in biophilic design. When an exceptional view is well framed — whereby space planning and furniture orientation encourage visual access to that view — artworks, biophilic or otherwise, are less likely to drive the experience of the space.

While art should not compete with quality views, it can be used to redirect attention to a preferred interior view when quality outdoor views are not available.

FIGURE 3.9. BIOPHILIC ART AND INSTALLATIONS.

IMPLEMENTATION PERSPECTIVES

CASE STUDY 3.1:
TACTILE MATERIALS IN PUBLIC SPACE

FIGURE 3.10 COOKFOX ARCHITECTS, BANK OF AMERICA TOWER AT ONE BRYANT PARK, NEW YORK CITY, USA, 2010. The biophilic experience of (a) the expansive main tower lobby, deliberately emphasises an intimate and tactile experience through choice materials, including (b) narrow oak entryway door handles; (c) visible fossils in Jerusalem stone; and (d) patina-inclined leather clad lift lobby.

Materials and finishes offer the possibility of transitioning from a visual to haptic experience. High-touch surfaces like doors, counters and furniture present an array of opportunities to enhance the occupant experience through biophilic goods and materials. The Bank of America Tower (Figure 3.10a) in New York City is a crystalline glass and steel composition rising from a granite pavement, and yet a visitor's first interaction is grasping the white oak handles of the lobby doors (Figure 3.10b).

Architect Rick Cook describes this as a deliberate biophilic experience: the oak handles, having a slightly coarse texture and narrow shaft, were selected as a tactile threshold in contrast with the tower. The core wall in the lobby is sheathed in Jerusalem stone (Figure 3.10c) with countless spiral ammonite fossils that children trace with their fingers. The walls of the lift lobby are clad in red leather (Figure 3.10d), intentionally selected as a warm contrast to the glass and steel that, after several years in place, has begun to show the patterns and patina of human touch.

With such a tall building, COOKFOX Architects' vision was to give the tower a human scale, allowing occupants to relate to the space. The biophilic materials selected helped to make that experience possible.

CASE STUDY 3.2:
GETTING FRACTALS RIGHT

The human brain subconsciously sorts between living and man-made items. An example would be our extreme sense of disappointment when we discover that something we thought was real turns out to be fake, such as a bouquet of flowers or a wood tabletop that upon closer inspection are discovered to be made of plastic.

Textile design in particular has long been inspired by patterns of flowers, leaves, trees, birds, seashells and other elements from nature. The transference of nature's likeness into design can be a powerful tool for connecting the occupant experience to the place. Representations and abstractions make the connection to nature without being fake.

In recent years, some designers have taken a more sophisticated approach to abstracting these representations of nature. Early adopters like David Oakie, of Pond Studios, created two very successful lines of carpet tiles for Interface, Human Nature and Urban Retreat (Figure 3.11a). Through colouration and three-dimensional patterning, these designs incorporate characteristics of moss and paving stones, abstracted enough to not be perceived as being a recreation of moss and stone. Other carpet tile manufacturers have attempted to mimic the success of Interface, yet by taking a more literal approach to representing nature, the result has been arguably less successful.

Mohawk launched a new line of carpet tiles called Relax (Figure 3.11b), which was the result of a design collaboration with fractal researcher Richard Taylor at the University of Oregon. Taylor and his team have been researching a concept called fractal fluency, which posits that because certain fractal ratios occur so frequently in nature, when we see them in human-designed objects, it is easier for the brain to process the images. This leads to measured drops in stress. The new Mohawk patterns are based on statistical fractals like the ones experienced in the dappled shadow patterns under some tree canopies.

FIGURE 3.11 EXPERIENCE OF CARPET DESIGN.
(a) 'Urban Retreat' carpet tiles by Interface are
analogous to moss and paving stones, visually
communicating a transition from one zone
to another; (b) 'Relax' carpet tiles by Mohawk
are based on statistical, mid-range fractals
(dimension = 1.3–1.5), considered the most
interesting and visually preferred; (c) arbitrary
or non-fractal designs are inherently less
capable of repeatedly capturing our interest and
thus tend to be less successful at contributing to
the biophilic experience.

CASE STUDY 3.3:
GOOD INTENTIONS GONE AWRY

Biophilic solutions that are coordinated with occupant behaviours are more likely to succeed. In a workplace example, frosted film on glass partitions was specified for conference rooms facing the communal lounge and kitchenette. The unfrosted organic shapes visually connected the two spaces. This solution had been selected as a way to balance privacy with daylight penetration to the conference room.

Although the design solution was considered cost-effective and biophilic, the user group had not been adequately understood. The design element was thus met with knavish subversion, whereby users wanting greater privacy covered the unfrosted shapes with dozens of Post-it notes (Figure 3.12).

Understanding occupant behaviours in advance of designing for them becomes even more essential when building in greater experiential distinctions, such as with biophilic design. In offices with differing levels of need to protect intellectual property or activity, a similar hierarchy of design solutions may be needed.

FIGURE 3.12 WORKPLACE CONFERENCE ROOM,
SILICON VALLEY, CALIFORNIA, USA, 2017.
Understanding the the necessary balance of
openness and privacy for a space is essential
to upholding a biophilic experience. In this
example, the see-through areas of a frosted glass
window were considered problematic and were
subsequently covered up.

CASE STUDY 3.4:
FLORA WITH AN ATTITUDE

Green walls can easily liven up an interior space, but some strategies are more effective than others at enhancing the biophilic experience. While a wall only of hardy pothos may be dramatic, it will not hold our attention and, over time, may come to be perceived as static. Monocultures do not occur frequently in nature, and often indicate a place that has been overrun by an invasive species. Biodiversity of planting in green walls gains viewer interest better than monocultures, possibly because they are perceived as being a living habitat and therefore an indication of a good place for other living things — in particular, people.

When thinking beyond the assortment of potted plants, indoor vegetation systems — whether as building systems–integrated, permanent/independent or modular/packaged — have varied benefits from a cost, maintenance and biophilic perspective. One solution may be more appropriate depending on the project goals, context and constraints.

In 2014, the Glumac engineering team deliberately introduced organic forms, ample daylight, outdoor access and a biodiverse indoor green wall (Figure 13.3a) to enliven their newly renovated office in Shanghai. After installation, the team discovered that their green wall was too close to the air vents, causing the plants to die back. The green wall was eventually replaced with a row of Sansevieria (Figure 13.3b), which have survived, but at the loss of biodiversity.

This story is not uncommon — plant species selection or placement is frequently misaligned with a project's air handling or electric lighting strategy. Interiorscaping relies on a balance of conditions and the benefits of biophilic greenery are but one of several considerations.

FIGURE 3.13 GENSLER, GLUMAC OFFICE, YUYUAN ROAD, SHANGHAI, CHINA, 2014. The Glumac office (a) shortly after opening and (b) the Sansevieria replacements are positioned to optimise visual access by occupants. Modular or packaged vegetated designs such as (c) the Verdure LIVE Moss Wellness Wall at the Bloomsday Cafe, in Philadelphia, Pennsylvania, USA, include custom lighting and watering, which may be an appropriate alternative for when building systems integration is not feasible.

CASE STUDY 3.5:
FAUNA WITH A CONTEMPLATIVE PRESENCE

In 2016, Sosolimited unveiled 'Diffusion Choir', a stunning computational, kinetic sculpture that simulates the collective movement of a flock of birds (Figure 3.14). The unique artwork, housed in a multi-story office building atrium, is made up of 400 folding 'birds' controlled by custom software running the Boids' 'flocking' algorithm. Designed to inspire calmness and collaboration, the installation uses the phenomenon of flocking birds as a metaphor for the client's core values — a spirit of innovation, collaboration and the concept that the capacity to accomplish great things is far greater as a group than individually.

With excellent lines of sight and daylight penetration, the atrium was a well-trafficked pathway, yet experientially deficient. The initial concept was to rehumanise the oversized space by enhancing the experience of the network of interior stairs by introducing sound masking in the form of a sculpture that could disappear and reappear out of thin air.

Sosolimited led the concept, physical design, animation design and programming, while Plebian Design and Hypersonic Engineering took on the mechanical and electrical design engineering and fabrication. There were some aesthetic challenges along the way and the sculptural composition went through several forms. The complexity and order of a rectilinear grid-like form was determined to work best for the software to express the natural visual curvature of flocking patterns. While speeding up the system would have better resembled a flock of birds, a slower motion was determined to be a unified solution that both acknowledged the limitations of the mechanics and provided the desired calming experience.

Over the course of each hour the 400 bird forms contract, disperse and, eventually, coalesce into a single entity, soaring through the atrium in fluid collaboration. In the end, the final design is nearly silent, so it is not a sound masking system, but the psychological effect it has in the atrium

FIGURE 3.14 SOSOLIMITED, DIFFUSION CHOIR, CAMBRIDGE, MASSACHUSETTS, USA, 2016. This awe-inspiring kinetic sculpture conveys the movement patterns of a flock of birds. The experience of the installation differs over the course of the day and the floor/level/height from which it is viewed.

is significant. The process for creating Diffusion Choir took two years from beginning to end. While wildly popular and exceptionally biophilic, Sosolimited co-founder Eric Gunther noted that planning for installations of this scale and complexity require considerable leeway and are best suited to long-term ownership or tenancy than for shorter-term tenancy.

CASE STUDY 3.6:
BRINGING WATER INDOORS

The presence of water in a building can create a memorable and pleasurable experience. The sound of water — like in a small stream, gentle waterfall or water wall — is an incredibly effective masking sound, not for its acoustic characteristics, but for the tendency of the brain to focus on that sound — a phenomenon known as psychoacoustics.

Acoustical design of water features is critical for optimising psychoacoustic comfort and experience. The American electronics company, Poly, discovered that in order for their indoor water feature to have a measurable positive impact on workplace experience, occupants needed to be able to both see and hear the water feature (Figure 3.15). However, running greater volumes of water was not a practical solution due to infrastructure and the spray/splash factor. The solution was for a tall water wall, visually accessible throughout the office, paired with audio broadcasting to reach occupants outside the immediate auditory proximity of the water feature.

FIGURE 3.15 ART AQUA, BIETIGHEIM, GERMANY. There are many ways to introduce water into indoor spaces, but vertical water walls make water more highly visible. The sight and sound of a water wall can be a powerful tool for masking distracting sounds in a workplace.

FIGURE 3.16 OPIARY INSTALLATION, BOUTIQUE DESIGN NEW YORK, JAVITS CONVENTION CENTER, NEW YORK CITY, USA, 2019. In an exploration of nature connectedness through texture, vegetation, form and water, this event installation brings together a suite of biophilic interior products without over-stimulating the user.

CHAPTER 4

IN THE HOME: CHERISHED RESIDENCES

FIGURE 4.1 VICTOR PIERRE HORTA, HOTEL
TASSEL, BRUSSELS, BELGIUM, 1895. In this
Art Nouveau townhouse, natural analogues are
expressed through the organic forms of the mural,
floor tiling, railing, columns and floral chandelier.

HISTORICAL CONTEXT

Biophilic design is not new. We can see homes designed by a number of well-known architects from the early twentieth century and earlier that can be characterised as biophilic. Sir John Soane played with surprising ways to bring light into a room, and created glimpses of adjoining spaces that compel visitors to continue their explorations of his home and museum in London. Victor Pierre Horta (Figure 4.1) and Antonio Gaudi used wildly biomorphic forms to animate their designs.

In one particular house, we can see the changing emotional state of an architect. Taliesin, built by Frank Lloyd Wright, is a home and architectural studio on the brow of a hill on his family's farm in Wisconsin, USA. Like many of his residential designs, it had a balance of prospect and refuge spaces. After the fire that was set in the murder of his mistress, Wright rebuilt a much more introspective house, dominated by refuge spaces. A few years later, when he was happily in a new relationship, an electrical fire destroyed a significant portion of Taliesin — this time he rebuilt with a balance of prospect and refuge spaces. Finally, when his architecture practice was booming, he constructed the bird walk, a bizarre narrow walkway cantilevered over the hillside, which added a strong perception of 'risk' to the experience of Taliesin.[1]

Biophilic homes, especially those built to suit, differ in character by building type and climate, as well as in the ways in which the resident spends their time while at home. Affordance theory postulates that spaces signal underlying psychological conditions to occupants — whether a home is convivial, reflective or reclusive. Where there is a desired balance of these conditions, biophilic homes have historically exhibited a balance of openness ('prospect') with opportunities for withdrawal ('refuge')and, sometimes, a little curiosity ('mystery') or sense of adventure ('risk').

DESIGN IMPACT OPPORTUNITY

Stephen Kellert, in his *Kinship to Mastery* (1997), observed that there is a progression in the nature bonding process. Pre-schoolers focus on attraction, desire, fear and aversion experiences with nature; children aged 6–9 transition to a more emotional relationship with nature; and at about 10 years old and onward, the relationship with nature becomes increasingly intellectual.[2] How that kinship plays out within the built environment depends on the biophilic experiences made available. For instance, research indicates that teenage girls with green space immediately outside their homes demonstrate better self-discipline (i.e. concentration, inhibition of initial impulses and delayed gratification) than those without.[3] Mastery of these personal skills often results in higher rates of professional, academic and personal success.

For young children, the home is the prime location for nurturing those experiential and emotional connections with nature. Opportunities for incorporating biophilic experiences will naturally vary depending on the home location, ownership structure and the designer's scope of work. In single-family residential buildings, the primary opportunities are with access to outdoor nature; the balancing of 'prospect' and 'refuge' spaces, such as with shared living spaces and reading nooks, respectively; the use of dynamic light, natural materials and biomorphic forms and patterns in furniture (Figure 4.2), hardware, fabrics and wall coverings (Figure 4.12) (see figure examples in Chapter 3).

FIGURE 4.2 KELLY HOPPEN INTERIORS, PRIVATE RESIDENCE, SOUTH WEST LONDON, UK, 2016. Stairwells can often be a challenge to gracefully integrate into an interiors strategy. Subtle infusions of nature in the iron banister form, waterfall chandelier and nature artworks tie the space together in a spatially dynamic vignette.

A biophilic design strategy for new multi-family residences can incorporate many strategies similar to a single-family home: outdoor space, a balanced floor plan and biophilic finishes. Unlike a single-family home, design solution replicability across units will make it easier to withstand quantity surveying or cost engineering exercises.

For renovations, the primary biophilic experiences are often limited to 'public' spaces and may also present a different value proposition to the owners than for tenants (see Chapter 2 on value proposition). Primary opportunities include visual and physical access to outdoor green spaces (Figure 4.11); prospect through the foyer, lobby, atrium, corridors, gym, terraces and similar spaces; the creation of convivial communal spaces through comfortable seating, a warm and welcoming materials palette, and an emphasis on community connectivity.

CASE STUDY 4.1:
THE COUNTRY HOME, NICHES AND INGLENOOKS

FIGURE 4.3 HELENA VAN VLIET ARCHITECT, PRIVATE RESIDENCE, BIRCHRUNVILLE, PENNSYLVANIA, USA, 2006. A variety of simple yet inviting refuge experiences offer protection overhead and at least one solid back surface, as well as (a,b,d) adjacency to operable windows, (a) integrated with ventilation, (d) privacy curtain and (a–d) task ambient lighting.

Large additions to older homes can often diminish the appeal of the original building. To hide the scale of the addition for a house in the countryside outside of Philadelphia, architect Helena van Vliet articulated the new construction into a series of smaller masses with an interior design strategy that reflects the idiom of the older structure.

van Vliet frequently uses spatial patterns like prospect and refuge to enrich the interior experience. She states, 'As a species, our lives occur in the balance between our urgent need for safety (refuge) and our yearning for exploration (prospect). All our projects honor and reflect this most profound of human patterns, which is deeply engrained in our shared evolutionary history. Overlooks, balconies, perches of any kind abound; alcoves, window seats and tucked away places affording beautiful sunny and far–away views.'[4]

The articulations of the addition helped to create a number of inviting inglenooks and window seats adjoining larger rooms (Figure 4.3). These spaces provide strong indoor refuge conditions while also framing great views, both inward to the rest of the living space and outward to the country landscape.

Each nook offers refuge without disconnecting the user from the larger space. As a biophilic theme, the series of nooks acknowledges the owner's prioritisation for layers of refuge that support key 'day in the life' activities, from reading or socialising to bathing and sleeping.

a

b

c

d

CASE STUDY 4.2:
THE HISTORIC ROWHOUSE, FIXTURES,
HARDWARE AND MEDALLIONS

FIGURE 4.4 PRIVATE RESIDENCE, MONTGOMERY STREET, JERSEY CITY, NEW JERSEY, USA, 2017. Fully renovated (a) master bath flooded with daylight, (b) second-floor bathroom scalloped sink and tropical wall covering, (c) rainfall shower heads, and (d, e) parlour floor bathroom ornate hardware. Hardware was hand selected by the owner with the intention of making each bathroom a unique experience.

The owners of this renovated three-storey, single-family c. 1864 brownstone wanted their new home to recapture the original details that had been stripped out over the years, while creating a launch point for incorporating more eclectic decorative items. The biophilic design strategy focused primarily on enriching the experience of the home through hardware, fixtures and wall coverings, with a particular emphasis on ceiling medallions and bathroom details. The living spaces have a sophisticated palette, whereas the bathrooms each balance a sense of otherworldliness with refinement and respite.

While the architect sourced the fixtures, the homeowners themselves sought out the balusters, hinges, light fixtures and doorknobs, visiting antique shops and internet sources over several months. This process required a considerable amount of personal time and patience. Finding hardware complementary to the time period meant identifying architectural salvage warehouses as well as companies that specialised in recreating antique products.

Finding ceiling medallions that they loved was difficult — products often appeared too generic for their eclectic home. They looked as far west as California, eventually finding an artist in San Francisco. At the artist's studio, they learned about the method and process behind making the medallions and acquired some fresh ideas for their renovation. After purchasing several medallions from the artist, they personally carried them on the plane back to New Jersey. The idiosyncratic nature of the effort expended to obtain those medallions, said the owner, has added a depth of appreciation and pride for their home.

FIGURE 4.5 PRIVATE RESIDENCE, MONTGOMERY STREET, JERSEY CITY, NEW JERSEY, USA, 2017. The biomorphic living room medallion, specially ordered to pair with the original 1860s medallion in the kitchen, is a focal point for the parlour floor. The globe pendant light was selected for economy and replaceability.

The master bathroom (Figure 4.4a) was expanded to take advantage of underutilised space as well as to maximise the view of the tree-canopied backyard from the bath and shower. The water closet features floor-to-ceiling jungle-patterned wall covering and a scalloped corner sink with exposed plumbing (Figure 4.4b) which allays the need for wall art. Additional biophilic features — dual waterfall showerheads (Figure 4.4c), a claw-foot bath, two sizes of classic honeycombed floor tiles, large potted plants and ample daylight — each add to the perception of being in a haven the owners described as being 'timeless, yet edgy and modern all at once'.

The parlour floor bathroom offers a more intimate experience both by necessity and by design. The cosy , windowless space is adorned with bold, floor-to-ceiling floral wall covering. Each piece of hardware is highly biophilic — attention is easily drawn to the ornate handles, hooks (Figure 4.4d) and door locks (Figure 4.4e).

The aesthetics and biophilic characteristics of the 1860s served as a guide for selecting the permanent house fixtures, while modern 'accessories' were selected for ease of replacement, should aesthetic preferences change over time. This was a strategy applied consistently throughout the house — very ornate medallions were offset with modern light fixtures (Figure 4.5) — to both manage costs and retain a degree of future flexibility.

Reflecting back on the process, the owner noted that one of the biggest lessons learned was that keeping a closer eye on the contractors might have better ensured that their original goal was honoured. While the owner had focused on salvaging existing treasures and replacing what was missing, it was hard to keep track of everything; the contractors discarded a few cherished items, including an ornate vent grate and one of the original, interior wooden doors, neither of which could be recovered.

CASE STUDY 4.3:
THE CITY HOME, ACCESS AND DIMENSIONS

Kelly Hoppen MBE's 650m^2 (7,000ft^2) family home boasts a large, open–plan, high–ceilinged living (Figure 4.6), dining and kitchen space, along with a breakfast nook and media room, designed to be open to or closed off from the main living area. Bedrooms feature a drop ceiling framing the bed and flanked by lighting that further encompasses the headboard in a refuge condition.

Hoppen's style — to create timeless and understated elegance while balancing Eastern principles on simplicity with Western aesthetics — fosters a biophilic experience through an emphasis on textures, quality daylight, the distribution of prospect and refuge throughout the residence and, perhaps most notably, through complexity and order of the floor plan, spatial volumes, furniture and other soft goods. Each room is designed to invite, captivate and intrigue by its art collection, indoor prospect and outdoor views. A neutral, calm colour palette was complemented by subdued, nature–inspired accent colours, while a mix of woods, metals, upholstery and decorative cushions enrich with visual intrigue and add greater dimension to the space.

When the project started, the challenge was to find a property with the right amount of daylight and manipulatable space to create the desired home experience. The property that was finally settled on was an empty shell, which presented a lot of opportunities for playing with volumes and to mediate daylight and perceptions of mystery, prospect and refuge. 'The volume of light and the sheer amount of space is very difficult to find, especially in London', notes Hoppen. '[Our home] has become a unique destination property'.[5]

FIGURE 4.6 KELLY HOPPEN INTERIORS, PRIVATE FAMILY RESIDENCE OF KELLY HOPPEN MBE, LONDON, UK, 2015. High ceilings and an open–plan design give flexibility to the space and encourage exploration, while a dining nook and media room provide retreat spaces along the perimeter.

CASE STUDY 4.4:
THE MULTI–FAMILY RESIDENCE,
AN EXERCISE IN REPOSITIONING

FIGURE 4.7 COOKFOX ARCHITECTS, MOOD BOARD FOR RENOVATION OF RESIDENTS' LOUNGE, ONE COLUMBUS PLACE, NEW YORK CITY, USA, 2016. This neutral colour palette assembles biophilic textures and materials to convey a calming feeling for a space to counter its frenetic urban location.

For the renovation of One Columbus Place — a 51–storey, 725–unit complex in Hell's Kitchen, New York City — the design team at COOKFOX Architects started by assessing opportunities available on site. At the first client meeting, experiential goals were discussed, before programming options, to ascertain how the design might achieve those goals.

The twin–towered building had an 84m^2 (905ft^2) party room and small sun deck for one of the towers and, on a different floor, a large terrace accessible from both towers. As a means to improve occupant access to nature, as well as to increase both real value to the client and hedonic value to current and prospective tenants, the design team proposed bringing the party room down to the terrace level and increasing its capacity to 200m^2 (2,160ft^2) to accommodate more activities. In doing so, the owner would need to agree to taking two of the terrace–adjacent residential units off the market.

Retrofits are often either focused on damage control and corrections or on adapting to a change in user needs or market demand. For architect Luca Baraldo, responding to a change in market demand often means identifying unique solutions to enhance the occupant experience and then having to create the argument for repurposing underutilised spaces, sometimes at a perceived expense. Proposing to take two units off the market presented one such scenario. For One Columbus Place, the client ran rough calculations and determined that the rent increase to compensate for the lost units would be modest and reasonable relative to comparable units in the neighbourhood.

The design team then began looking at finish materials, always taking a sensorial approach and starting with natural materials like wood and stone. Furniture, wall coverings and material patterns were explored next

FIGURE 4.8 THE RESIDENTIAL TOWER LOBBY AT ONE COLUMBUS PLACE, NEW YORK CITY, USA. (a) before renovation, Buck/Cane Architects with SLCE Architects, 1999, and (b) after renovation, COOKFOX Architects, 2018. The redesign of the lobby intentionally used a biophilic lens to change the entrance experience. The procession and lighting in the updated design better support wayfinding and prospect through the space; the seating area is more inviting, supporting social interaction and, while both lobbies have a wood finish, the COOKFOX design shows the wood grain, giving the space a warmer, welcoming feel.

(Figure 4.7). Consideration was given to natural imperfections, the story of the material, its impact on other project goals and its contribution to the narrative of the space, which was an important step in ensuring a biophilic experience. Only after this research was a material presented to the client.

After renovation, which included the lobby (Figure 4.8), lounge (Figure 4.9) and sun deck (Figure 4.10), as well as the terrace, gym and basketball court, units were able to command upper-tier, market-rate rental numbers.[6]

FIGURE 4.9 THE RESIDENTS' LOUNGE AT ONE COLUMBUS PLACE, NEW YORK CITY, NEW YORK, USA. (a) before renovation, 84m^2 (905ft^2), and (b) after renovation, 200m^2 (2,160ft^2), COOKFOX Architects, 2018. The redesign and expansion of the lounge replaced uniform lighting with task lighting, a warm colour and materials palette of wood and leather, several distinct but flexible activity zones, and direct visual and physical access to the building's main landscaped terrace.

FIGURE 4.10 THE FIFTH–FLOOR SUN DECK AT
ONE COLUMBUS PLACE, NEW YORK CITY, USA.
(a) before renovation and (b) after renovation,
COOKFOX Architects, 2018. The redesign of the
sun deck sought to introduce greater variation in
refuge characteristics — space, shade, seating,
view aperture — and to more dynamically connect
users with nature.

FIGURE 4.11 ATELIERS JEAN NOUVEL, ONE CENTRAL PARK, 28 BROADWAY, CHIPPENDALE, SYDNEY, AUSTRALIA, 2013. As an urban renewal project, the integrated landscape and architecture uses vertical plantings, designed by Patrick Blanc, to adorn approximately 50% of the façade. The horizontal planters allow a view to nature for every residence while doubling as sun shades for the units below.

FIGURE 4.12 PRIVATE RESIDENCE, BEDMINSTER, NEW JERSEY, USA, C. 1960–2018. A landscape mural adorns the two–storey entry stair of a 1790s farmhouse. First painted in the 1960s, the mural continues to retain an emotional connection to the landscape, despite the change in ownership over time. In the 1960s an artist added the owner and his son standing on the cliff (top centre) and in 2018, when a crack in the plaster was being repaired, the most recent owner had his two hunting dogs and a covey of quail added (bottom left).

CHAPTER 5

IN THE SCHOOL: SUPPORTIVE LEARNING

FIGURE 5.1 DEANE & WOODWARD, COLUMN CAPITALS OF OXFORD UNIVERSITY MUSEUM, PARKS ROAD, OXFORD, UK, 1860. The intricate flora and fauna motifs carved by Irish masons O'Shea and Whelan for the interior column capitals were influenced by the writings and consultation of John Ruskin, whose works emphasised connections between nature, art and society. Ruskin's perspectives have regained popularity in this new era of environmentalism, sustainability and craftsmanship.

HISTORICAL CONTEXT

Throughout history, 'learning from nature' has been a recurring theme. Nature as a setting in which to learn more traditional subjects is somewhat of a new idea.

The German kindergarten (or 'garden for the children') as an educational setting is a powerful metaphor. In 1837, German pedagogue Friedrich Fröbel wanted to nurture young children as one would nurture young plants in a garden. This grew out of his experience of spending much of his childhood in a garden.[1]

Schools at the turn of the twentieth century were day–lit and naturally ventilated by operable windows. This typically allowed for views to trees, clouds and other outside activity. In the 1960s, the US education system perpetuated the belief that views were 'distractions' and that the attention of children should be focused on activities within the classroom. Henceforth, the construction of windowless or transom–window classrooms became pervasive in practice, particularly among temporary modular structures, many of which are still in use decades later.

Ornamental column capitals, cornices, mouldings and other architectural elements — interior connections to nature that are characteristic of historic institutional structures such as at Oxford University (Figure 5.1) — also fell out of favour in the twentieth century.

Today, ornamentation is experiencing a resurgence. The green building movement has helped to bring daylight back into school design, initially as an energy conservation strategy, and evidence continues to indicate that daylighting classrooms can lead to better test scores.[2 3] And rather than being a distraction, research suggests that views of nature can support longer attention spans.[4] While test scores are often touted as the for biophilic views in educational settings, lower blood pressure and stress levels, better mood and short–term memory are also valid motivators.[5] The health outcomes are immediate benefits, while improved test scores are longer–term benefits.

DESIGN IMPACT OPPORTUNITY

Nature serves as a supportive environment for cognitive development and performance, from early childhood through adulthood. Greater exposure to nature is shown to have a significant positive association with school experience, subsequent graduation rates and the plans of students to attend college or university,[6] which influence an individual's economic and social outcomes later in life.

Allowing children to play and learn in nature can provide benefits like mental restoration, better behaviour and enhanced focus. Access to nature while school is in session has been shown to positively impact overall cognitive development, particularly the working memory and attention of students.[7]

Within the classroom, extensive research shows that daylight and views to nature are considered to have the greatest impact for cognitive development and performance. Quality daylight and views help improve attendance and test scores and support health,[8,9] reduce off-task behaviour and improve classroom engagement. Other researched benefits include faster recovery from stressful experiences and increased attentional function and exhibit significantly less life stress.[13]

David Orr, Emeritus Professor of Environmental Studies at Oberlin College, says that buildings inherently tell us about the belief systems that led to their design — they are 'crystallised pedagogy'.[14] Biophilic design can be leveraged as a philosophy of education and design that both helps support improved academic performance and a greater connectedness with buildings and nature (Figures 5.2 and 5.6).

FIGURE 5.2 FARMING ARCHITECTS, VAC LIBRARY, HANOI, VIETNAM, 2018. As a community amenity, this outdoor educational environment integrates learning and playing with production systems including horticulture, aquaculture and animal husbandry. Exploration, experimentation and knowledge sharing can be shared with the neighbourhood, creating a knowledge base that would not be otherwise gained from book study.

CASE STUDY 5.1:
RE-ENVISIONING THE LEARNING OPPORTUNITY

FIGURE 5.3A–C CRAIG GAULDEN DAVIS ARCHITECTS, GREEN STREET ACADEMY CLASSROOM REDESIGN CONCEPT, BALTIMORE, MARYLAND, USA, 2018/19. Comparative classroom study sites included two maths classrooms: (a) proposed biophilic classroom incorporating four simple design interventions; (b) the control classroom; and (c) the biophilic classroom.

The Green Street Academy is a locally funded public charter school in Baltimore, using a STEAM (Science, Technology, Engineering, Arts, Mathematics) curriculum. The selected location for the school was in a shuttered public school building in an under-served neighbourhood. The 1925-era school was renovated and redesigned by architect Jim Determan of Craig Gaulden Davis Architects. Biophilic additions included indoor koi ponds, greenhouses and artwork of local ecosystems. While the classrooms were not designed with specific biophilic elements, many are located on the long, east-facing rear façade, with a view out to grass and distant trees. The glare from the morning sun causes teachers to lower the window blinds, which are then rarely lifted.

Determan wanted to explore whether the use of low-cost biophilic interior elements would both lower the stress and improve learning outcomes in a classroom (Figure 5.3a). To test Determan's hypothesis, a sixth-grade maths classroom was renovated with carpet tiles, window blinds, a wallpaper frieze and waveform ceiling tiles, each expressing biomorphic forms or complex fractal patterns (Figure 5.3c). The auto-controlled fabric window blinds lifted, once the morning glare was off the windows, to a view of a newly planted outdoor garden. For comparison, in a seventh-grade maths classroom on the same hall (Figure 5.3b), carpet tiles without any biophilic references were laid to match the acoustic and haptic experiences of the biophilic classroom.

Classes held at the same time in the two classrooms were used for biometric testing. As heart rate variability (HRV) is a good indicator of the ability to recover from stress (high HRV is generally considered healthy), student stress levels were measured — at the beginning and end of class, three times per week — using a finger-clip HRV monitor synced with a smartphone app.

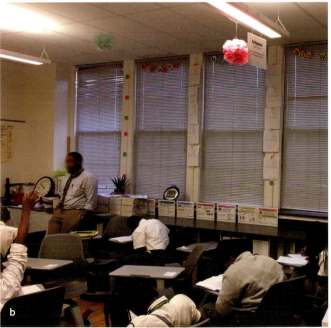

During the 2018/19 school year, the experiment tracked academic performance in the sixth-grade maths class. Test scores of current students were compared to those of students in the prior year in the same classroom with the same teacher and same curriculum (Figure 5.3c). Due to the difficulty in getting permissions to conduct biometric testing with schoolchildren, only four months of HRV data are available (Figure 5.3d).

Previously, the walls were covered with papers displaying formulas and notes, which some teachers use to signal how much content is being conveyed in their classroom. Neuroscientist Thomas Albright argues that covering the walls with so much material can result in an overstimulated environment.

Getting the teacher to agree to limit the amount of material taped onto the walls in the biophilic classroom was a challenge. At first the teacher felt that this would limit the students' retention of lessons, agreeing to put up papers temporarily and then take them down. Over time, the teacher came to realise that the students behaved more calmly in the room, she felt calmer in the room, and that other teachers would come into the room to take a break.

The view out of the window could have been a significant factor in the outcomes. However, for most of the experiment there were no leaves on the trees. As seen in the HRV data (Figure 5.3d), in April when the trees blossomed there was a spike in the response, which then diminished after the bloom. This is a strong indication that the biophilic design elements within the room were the significant factor in the outcomes.[15]

d

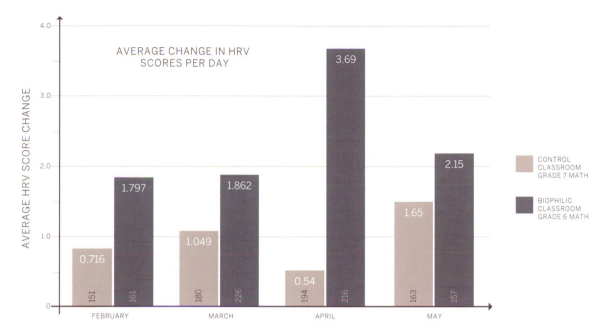

AVERAGE CHANGE IN HRV
SCORES PER DAY

AVERAGE HRV SCORE CHANGE

FEBRUARY · MARCH · APRIL · MAY

0.716 · 1.797 · 1.049 · 1.862 · 0.54 · 3.69 · 1.65 · 2.15

151 · 161 · 180 · 226 · 194 · 216 · 163 · 157

CONTROL
CLASSROOM
GRADE 7 MATH

BIOPHILIC
CLASSROOM
GRADE 6 MATH

e

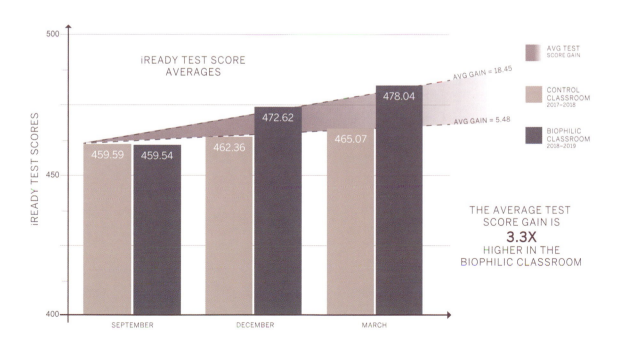

iREADY TEST SCORE
AVERAGES

iREADY TEST SCORES

SEPTEMBER · DECEMBER · MARCH

459.59 · 459.54 · 462.36 · 472.62 · 465.07 · 478.04

AVG GAIN = 18.45
AVG GAIN = 5.48

AVG TEST
SCORE GAIN

CONTROL
CLASSROOM
2017–2018

BIOPHILIC
CLASSROOM
2018–2019

THE AVERAGE TEST
SCORE GAIN IS
3.3X
HIGHER IN THE
BIOPHILIC CLASSROOM

CASE STUDY 5.2:
REPURPOSING FOR DIVERSITY AND INCLUSION

FIGURE 5.4 OLIVER HEATH DESIGN, THE GARDEN SCHOOL, HACKNEY, UK, 2018. The new playroom employs simple carpeted cubby refuges, fractal patterned carpet, tactile nature objects, and views to the adjacent outdoor playground to connect the children to their peers and landscaped outdoors.

Running around in a schoolyard can give a direct connection to nature and is great fun for most children. While there is evidence that contact with nature is beneficial for children on the autism spectrum[16] the scrum of the playground can be overstimulating.

Architect Oliver Heath worked with the Garden School Hackney to convert an underutilised, wedge-shaped storage room into a space for students with autism (Figure 5.4). The intent was to create a space that was calming, yet still encouraged play and interaction without disconnecting the kids from their classmates and schoolyard. The crux of the design challenge was to moderate stimuli while keeping the space interesting. Heath said 'We were careful to talk to the school, the teachers' and others, also noting that the children can be very particular about what stimulates them, which added a level of complexity to the design process. Hexagonal pods were created for the children to both crawl into and see out of to the rest of the space. Heath said that it took some effort to determine the right size of the pods so that they felt embracing but not confining — a considerable amount of time was spent sitting under desks, raising and lowering them to test right height of pods, changing the acoustics of the spaces and gazing out toward the windows to get a true sense of the spaces he was creating.

The Interface carpet tiles display abstractions of natural patterns and colours — earth tones, greens and others — that would be pleasing but not overwhelming. Douglas fir panelling was selected for its wide grain structure to heighten the visual and tactile experience. Window seats were designed to offer a sense of prospect out to the trees and schoolyard but without the anxiety. Finally, the forest mural adds some depth to the small space.

Teachers later reported that the children immediately felt very comfortable upon entering the room and frequently interact with each other in a peek-a-boo manner from the refuge pods — the most popular feature of the room.

CASE STUDY 5.3:
DESIGN THAT INFORMS CURRICULUM

For much of the twentieth century the focus of mechanical engineering had been to produce spaces that achieved uniform temperature, airflow and humidity levels. Lighting design was similarly focused on providing uniform light levels throughout a space. However, humans did not evolve in controlled uniform environments, and students seem to perform better in classrooms that have a variety of thermal and light conditions within the space.[17]

At De Montfort University in Leicester, UK, the Schools of Engineering are housed in the naturally ventilated, day–lit Queen's Building (Figure 5.5). Some of the interior spaces are as complex as those created by deconstructivists, but the forms are the result of three–dimensional modelling to induce airflows and capture daylight. Mechanical engineering students are studying in a building that does not have fans, pumps and metal ductwork — the building fabric itself replaces those components. Airflows are variable, but temperatures always remain within acceptable ranges. Sunlight and shadows move through the building, adding intrigue to the fine–grained patterns of the interior brickwork.

Quantity surveying or cost estimating was challenging for the contractors as typical mechanical systems were eliminated and replaced by brickwork that was both structural and served as ventilation shafts.[18] Substantial testing occurred after completion to prove that the building was performing as intended.

Students and faculty still actively monitor the performance of the building, and the Institute for Energy and Sustainable Development is now located in the building. The Queen's Building is a rare example of an academic building that is itself a teaching tool. While not overtly biophilic, it provides an experience that connects students with natural systems.

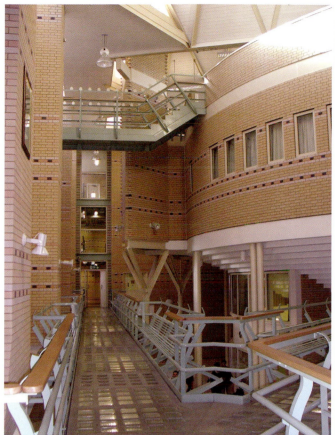

FIGURE 5.5 SHORT AND ASSOCIATES, QUEEN'S
BUILDING, DE MONTFORT UNIVERSITY,
LEICESTER, UK, 1993. The day–lit and naturally–
ventilated central circulation area, with bond–
patterned brick and a balance of prospect and
risk, creates a subtle yet enduring biophilic
experience within this 1995 RIBA Award recipient.

FIGURE 5.6 IBUKU, GREEN SCHOOL, ABIANSEMAL, BALI, INDONESIA, 2008–19. Recipient of the 2019 Stephen R. Kellert Biophilic Design Award, Green School Bali combines vernacular architecture with a comprehensive green education programme for a holistic biophilic experience: (a) the inviting, open-air concept immerses students in nature; (b) prospect and refuge are essential experiences; (c) complexity and order can be found throughout the school, guiding students from space to space; (d) the various classroom configurations each emphasise the experience of bamboo, daylight and outdoor views; (e) an enduring connection to place is fortified in the building structure; and (f) the bamboo cathedral central to the school is inspired by the Fibonacci sequence and spiralling nautili. The draw of this holistic educational experience has led to the development of green schools in New Zealand, South Africa and Mexico.

IN THE STORE: ENTICING RETAIL

FIGURE 6.1 ERNEST GEORGE & PETO, THOMAS GOODE & CO., MAYFAIR, LONDON, UK, 1891/2009. Fine bone china and porcelain retailer Thomas Goode and Company have occupied this Queen Anne-style building for over 100 years, showcasing the same product for which the space was initially built. The rear showroom, day-lit with high ceilings, presents a complex but orderly array of fine bone china and porcelain in a dining-ready setting that draws customers in to explore and imagine.

HISTORICAL CONTEXT

Retail spaces — whether instinctively, haphazardly or technocratically — have capitalised on our innate affinity for the savannah-like environments of our early Homo sapien ancestors.[1] Clustered trees, semi-open spaces, refuge from sun, heat, rain and camaraderie, distinct installations such as water features, dense vegetation, multiple-view corridors and high levels of visual access can all be found in shopping malls around the world. These design gestures have measurable influence over consumer purchasing habits that can help retail stakeholders capture greater profits.[2]

Designer department store Liberty of London's 1924 Tudor Revival style building was an early take on themed immersive retail, differentiating itself from contemporaries by aligning experiential qualities of the retail venue with customer service to elevate the whole customer experience. This perspective on competitive advantage has trickled down from malls to department stores to flagship stores to pop-up shops. Thomas Goode and Company's flagship store in London (Figure 6.1) offers high, canopy-like ceilings, daylight and perceptions of prospect and mystery across its sales floors with well-appointed displays conveying a desirable space — one in which customers could imagine themselves having a dinner party.

In contrast, the biophilic experience in recent decades has been largely intermingled with light quality, daylighting and energy efficiency initiatives. The Greenwich Millenium Village London location of Sainsbury's, with its biomorphic ceiling of clerestory windows (Figure 6.2), was an early example.

Unit sales is an industrial-age metric for store productivity. Now more than ever brick and mortar retail is about the customer experience. This pertains to services as well as brand and product engagement through cultural and emotional connectivity — visceral experiences that cannot be replicated online. Biophilic design presents a lens for crafting bespoke multisensory customer experiences — and 'experience per square foot', as projected by KPMG, will be a key performance indicator used by retail brands in the coming years.[3]

DESIGN IMPACT OPPORTUNITY

The transient nature of retail, especially in malls, department stores and other consolidated retail venues such as transit hub concession areas, means that there is a limited window of opportunity to capture the attention of a prospective customer and to draw them in. Sweeping architectural gestures, mood lighting, music and air conditioning can be effective, as can a lingering scent from essential oils and the information richness of a window dressing or product display. Each of these methods are opportunities for incorporating biophilic design, not just to lure customers, but to increase enticement, dwell times and purchases and, ultimately, to create a memorable experience that encourages return patronage, brand loyalty and positive social media behaviour.

A basic tenant of retail design is that the longer someone spends in store the more likely they are to make a purchase. The use of living elements in display windows can increase the amount of time gaze is captured and the number of people who are likely to enter a shop.[4] Partially revealed views — the 'mystery' condition — can induce exploration and increase the likelihood of drawing people through a space.[5]

Daylight and greenery in retail venues are known to contribute to employee workplace satisfaction and positive public perception of a brand, as well as to increased foot traffic, dwell time and pricing. The inclusion of skylights has been credited with yielding statistically significant increases in sales per square metre in both grocery and clothing stores.[6][7] Research also suggests a 15–25% increase in the hedonic value of goods sold in well-vegetated shopping environments.[8]

Themed environments and immersive retail present opportunities to elevate the consumer—brand relationship from being transactional to relational. Immersive retail engages customer senses to transport them to a time, place or experience that inspires a memorable relationship or connection to place.

FIGURE 6.2 SAINSBURY'S NEAR GREENWICH
MILLENNIUM VILLAGE, LONDON, UK, C. 2000.
The experimental prototype grocery store focused
on a daylighting design including an undulating,
biomorphic shell for bringing light in to create
a dramatic space. To keep the ceiling lines
pristine, the ventilation system was integrated
with an underfloor air delivery system under the
kickplates of display racks. There was significant
public outcry when this store was demolished to
make way for new development.

CASE STUDY 6.1:
REPURPOSING OF AN HISTORIC BUILDING

FIGURE 6.3 INTERFACE SHOWROOM AT MIES VAN DER ROHE BUSINESS PARK, KREFELD, GERMANY, 2016. Beyond the reception counter stands a water wall intended to engender calm and curiosity. The uninterrupted sequence draws people through the space and down the stairs to the showroom. The water wall can be experienced from a seated position at multiple vantage points on both the upper and lower levels of the building.

Ludwig Mies van der Rohe designed only one industrial zone. In 2016, the former porter's lodge at the Mies van der Rohe Business Park in Krefeld, Germany, became the new home to carpet tile company, Interface (Figure 6.3). Natural spatial patterns including prospect, refuge and mystery, as well as maintaining quality daylight, were identified early in the design process as a conceptual framework for the interior design. While the building exterior and landscape held historic designation prohibiting modification, the design team had free rein to demolish the many interior dividing walls that had been added in the decades since the original 1930s construction. The return to an open plan, more in line with the original space, better supported Interface's goal to provide both flexible and collaborative workspace and areas of retreat for tasks that necessitated focused attention.

Realisation that the 650m^2 (6,997ft^2), one-storey building would not be adequate space to serve the myriad activities of a showroom and office, led to the basement being incorporated into the programme design. The design challenge was to find a way to draw clientele down to the basement level showroom without making them feel disconnected from the outdoors.

The initial approach was to animate the space by digging out one of the basement walls to create a lowered terrace. In the design process, the historic designation was discovered to be inclusive of the basement walls — an architectural solution was off the table; the design challenge had to be met with an interior design solution.

The final solution was to create a central stairway with a floor-to-ceiling water wall, physically starting from the ceiling of the main level and extending down to the stair landing at the lower level — visible from several vantage points on both levels. The sight and sound of the water wall was intended both to relax full-time employees and to draw clients through the space and from one floor to the next.

CASE STUDY 6.2:
EXPRESSING PRODUCT ORIGIN

FIGURE 6.4 KD ONE, INNISFREE, UNION SQUARE, NEW YORK CITY, NEW YORK, USA, 2017. The second-floor office, floating over the reception counter, features operable windows giving the illusion that the customers are in a garden looking towards a home or, from inside, occupants are looking 'outside' into the garden.

Retail brands such as South Korea–based skincare company Innisfree, have leveraged biophilic design to promote a memorable customer experience and reinforce their brand identity. Innisfree's flagship store in Myeonngdong Seoul was designed by SOFTlab to captivate shoppers with indoor greenery, multisensory art and natural material use. At this location, 'The Cloud,' an art installation by Richard Clarkson, interacts with customers as they move through the store, by flashing lightning and thunder in response to a person's proximity. Customisable fragrance diffusers further immerse customers. The success of the flagship store design was inspiration for other Innisfree locations to apply biophilic design.

The New York City Union Square location (Figure 6.4) showcases a 169m^2 (1,824ft^2) green wall that spans 21m (70ft) long and 7.3m (24ft) high with nearly 10,000 plants. What makes it biophilic is not as much the scale of the green wall, but its species diversity — there are 11 different varieties of tropical plants — and the connection of vegetation to the products' origin story. The green wall plantings continue from ceiling to floor, behind a partially transparent display and can be experienced from both the ground level sales floor and the office cantilevered over the register counter which, in contrast, features digitised landscape images.

CASE STUDY 6.3:
DISCOVERING IMMERSIVE DESIGN
THROUGH COLLABORATION

In an idiosyncratic play, counter to coffee-shop culture, the expansive entry-to-exit sequence of Seesaw Coffee's Chaoyang Joycity location definitively contributed to an immersive, biophilic guest experience.

The goal for Seesaw Coffee and the nota architects design team was to provide 'coffee experiences' through the convergence of quality coffee beans and distinct design in a way that encouraged the confluence of people from all walks of life. Positioned in a bookstore on the top level of a mall in Beijing, this boutique coffee shop needed to feel independent from the bookstore, yet fully merged with the interior landscape. The unique, pre-existing characteristics of the available space, including varied floor elevations, offered programming challenges and design opportunities.

Scale, orientation, comfort and other factors were considered for attracting a varied clientele while optimising the perception of safety among patrons. By making use of the pre-existing, split-level layout, the design team was able to create a sunken plaza. Through materiality and ambience, a garden concept materialised.

Stepped platforms supported seating and a hut-like coffee bar. Wood blocks and planters were customised as variable-height seat backings and dividers to complement the assortment of floor levels and terrain within the surrounding landscape. Density and height of seating and vegetation was aimed at providing degrees of prospect and refuge for group and private conversation, observation and contemplation. The design strategy also included an assortment of table lamps and landscape lighting for wayfinding.

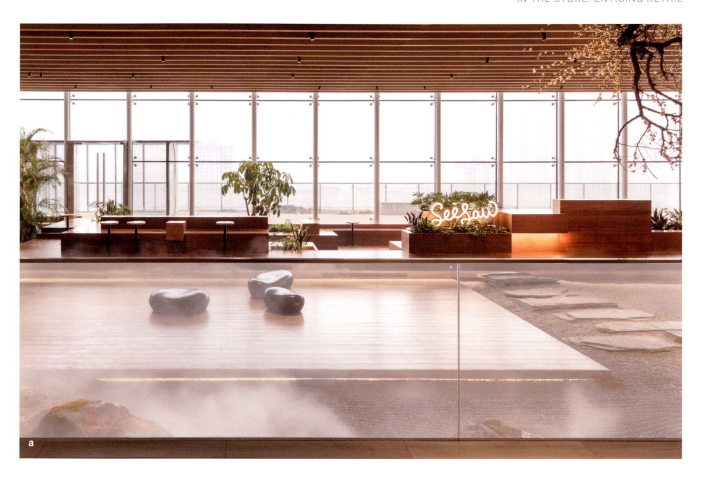

FIGURE 6.5A NOTA ARCHITECTS, SEESAW
COFFEE, CHAOYANG JOYCITY, BEIJING, CHINA,
2018. The coffee shop becomes the destination
as customers descend from the bookstore, move
along a stepping stone path, through the misty
sunken plaza, to the coffee bar. The proximity to
the floor-to-ceiling glass curtain wall creates the
illusion of being in a larger space.

b

FIGURE 6.5B–C NOTA ARCHITECTS, SEESAW COFFEE, CHAOYANG JOYCITY, BEIJING, CHINA, 2018. Approaching Seesaw, (b) views to seating areas are slowly revealed as customers meander through the space. Wood seating, tables and decking are suggestive of being in a casual outdoor space; and (c) the split–level design provides prospect over an earthen terrain, while pockets of vegetation contribute to the intimacy and perception of being in a garden.

In a collaboration between the coffee shop design team and the designers of the surrounding bookstore interior and landscape design, — Coba Design Qide Song and CN Flower Zongyong Ling, respectively — an ephemeral, multisensory experience emerged. Perimeter vegetation and coarse terrain alongside the pathway to the coffee shop enhanced the perception of entering a floating garden. To meet the growth demand of the mossy landscape, it was determined that routine moisture management would be necessary. Misting devices were incorporated into the design with the scheduled release of mist into the space twice daily. This mechanical solution subsequently became a defining enhancement to the perception of a floating garden, replete with intimacy, mystery, water, and a truly unique coffee experience.

FIGURE 6.6 BACKEN, GILLAM & KROEGER,
RESTORATION HARDWARE, THE GALLERY
AT THE ESTATE IN BUCKHEAD, ATLANTA,
GEORGIA, USA, 2014. Designed as a 'destination
for inspiration', (a) RH's dramatic central stairwell
creates an engaging experience of risk/peril; and
(b) the combination of canopy beds, refuge chairs
and dramatic lighting invite exploration.

FIGURE 6.7 DARTBROOK RUSTIC GOODS, KEENE,
NEW YORK, USA. Replete with handcrafted
furniture and goods made from locally–
sourced and natural materials or inspiration,
the Dartbrook immersive retail experience
encourages customers to explore the many rooms
and envision their ideal living spaces.

CHAPTER 7

IN THE OFFICE:
FOCUSED AND CREATIVE WORKSPACES

FIGURE 7.1 FRANK LLOYD WRIGHT, JOHNSON WAX / S C JOHNSON AND SON ADMINISTRATION BUILDING, RACINE, WISCONSIN, USA, 1934. The columns of abstracted trees — creating a canopy effect over the workspace while maintaining excellent prospect throughout the space — makes for a fantastic savannahh analogue. The space is so well loved by users that 80 years on it remains intact with its original design.

HISTORICAL CONTEXT

The workplace has seen a drastic transformation from the boys' club of the 1950s, to the cubicle fields of the 1980s and the open plans of the 2000s. This transformation has paradoxically been likened to the evolution of zoo design, each cubicle likened to an animal cage, except that place design for zoo animals to socialise, hunt and rest is decades ahead of place design for people to collaborate, work and restore.

Exceptions to this comparison have been exalted for their ingenuity in designing for human habitat. The savannahh–like interior of Frank Lloyd Wright's Johnson Wax building (Figure 7.1) is one enduring example. Others have recorded financial savings and bolstered brand recognition from making drastic improvements to human habitability. In 1978, ING Bank directors shared a vision for a new 49,982m^2 (538,000ft^2) headquarters in Amsterdam. The focus of the building design was to maximise natural lighting, integrate organic art and install water features to enhance worker productivity and create a new image for the bank. After the relocation, absenteeism decreased by 15% and employees reportedly looked forward to coming to work and voluntarily tended to the planted vegetation features in the building.[1] In addition to saving an estimated £1.3 million (US$2.6 million) per year in operation costs from their new energy system and daylighting strategies, the new headquarters refreshed ING's image in Holland as a progressive and creative bank.[2]

For most adults, the workplace is where substantial daytime hours are spent. Companies aim for their employees to be fully engaged and productive, but often work environments do not support those outcomes. Lowered productivity can stem from noise distraction, attention fatigue, lack of sleep and bad moods.[3] The physical workplace can either amplify or dampen many of the underlying factors of productivity.

DESIGN IMPACT OPPORTUNITY

In all sectors, efforts to reduce absenteeism and presenteeism by even a fraction of a percent can yield substantial financial benefits for an organisation.

Exposure to real nature enables better focus, mental stamina and productivity. Strategic workstation orientation emphasising a view to nature can have economic value relative to worker performance, with long-term productivity improvements yielding increased profits.[4][5] View and daylight quality can significantly affect how employees behave — where they work, eat and break,[6] as well as how much time is spent working while at the office and sleeping at home.[7][8]

Noise induced distraction has significant quantifiable negative impacts on ideation, reading comprehension, logical reasoning and useful interpretation of long-term memories.[9][10][11][12][13] Attaching positive subjective meaning to the aural workplace experience can help combat noise distraction and associated health impacts. Nature-inspired acoustic treatments and water soundscapes can be incorporated to improve task performance and positive employee perception of well-being.[14]

A holistic biophilic workplace design strategy recognises well-being as the aggregate of all our senses — visual, aural, gustatory, olfactory, tactile, temporal, etc. Our judgement of tranquillity relies on the harmonisation of sensory inputs,[15] which may differ among user groups. Emphasis on effective daylighting, thoughtful spatial configurations, a multisensory experience and, when possible, natural ventilation strategies, interior greenery and ample views to nature, create dynamic and healthful workplace experiences.

FIGURE 7.2 CAMENZIND EVOLUTION WITH HENRY J LYONS, GOOGLE DOCKS, BARROW STREET, DUBLIN, IRELAND, 2012. The design intent for this Platinum–certified LEED for Commercial Interiors building was to deliver a space that didn't feel like an office but more like a home away from home. One of many biophilic interventions in the building, this space offers two different experiences of prospect and refuge without disconnecting occupants from the broader workplace community.

CASE STUDY 7.1:
THE EVOLUTION OF A DESIGN STUDIO – 6TH AVENUE

The biophilic workplace narrative for COOKFOX Architects began in 2006, when they signed a lease for 641 Sixth Avenue in New York City. Originally the penthouse restaurant for a department store, the 1,126m^2 (12,121ft^2) space had a 6m high ceiling and a curving façade recessed from the building parapet. The prior tenant had lined the perimeter with enclosed offices and filled the space with high–partitioned cubicles (Figure 7.3a), severely obstructing views and daylight penetration.

Wanting to recapture the potential for deep daylight and prospect views through the space and to the city, COOKFOX designed for built low partitions (107cm), giving almost every workstation a view to curving windows and the adjoining roof (Figure 7.3b). The original Ionic column details were refurbished and a simple materials palette was specified to emphasise natural textures, patterns and colours, as well as sustainability. Strand board, bamboo plywood, paper resin counters and the first–ever, non–repeating patterned carpet tiles from Interface were among the most prominent materials used.

Once settled in their office, employees installed a 334m^2 (3,600ft^2) green roof. With minimal maintenance of the eight sedum species, native grasses colonised the roof, followed by insects, dragonflies, small birds and eventually kestrels. Daily, office–wide exposure to this biodiversification shifted perceptions of the green roof from being a decorative experiment to a living ecosystem. Workplace pride increased, vegetable plantings and apiaries were added, and honey harvesting flourished.

FIGURE 7.3A–B COOKFOX ARCHITECTS, SIXTH AVENUE, NEW YORK CITY, USA, 2006. In stark contrast to the prior tenant conditions (a), the Platinum-certified LEED for Commercial Interiors renovation emphasised views, daylight, historic ornamental preservation and (b) views to a 334m² green roof that became the office's signature feature.

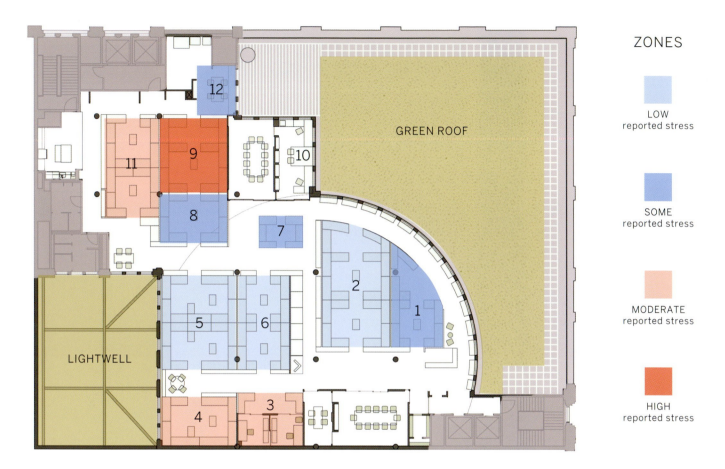

ZONES

LOW
reported stress

SOME
reported stress

MODERATE
reported stress

HIGH
reported stress

GREEN ROOF

LIGHTWELL

FIGURE 7.3C COOKFOX ARCHITECTS, POST–OCCUPANCY STRESS MAP, SIXTH AVENUE, NEW YORK CITY, USA, 2014. The floor plan documents feedback on employee stress by work zone, indicating the highest reports of stress occurring in zone 9 (in orange), which was the only zone with no direct view to the outside, and was near to sources of heightened noise distraction, i.e. kitchen, printers and exit.

While the space was well loved and shared — as a commercial film set and *National Geographic*® magazine cover photo — post–occupancy evaluations revealed another story. The office severely lacked refuge spaces and it was impacting workplace stress and productivity (Figure 7.3c). The workforce of 70 was limited to two conference rooms and two small communal tables. Employees ate lunch at their desks and often resorted to the fire escape stairwells to make phone calls. With a 10–year lease on the verge of expiration, COOKFOX began thinking about how to achieve a better balance of prospect and refuge in their office of the near future.

CASE STUDY 7.2:
THE EVOLUTION OF A DESIGN STUDIO – 57TH STREET

On the hunt for a new home, COOKFOX's real estate broker, CBRE, was tasked with finding a space with four key experiential priorities: ample daylight, capacity to house 100 occupants on a single floor, occupiable terrace(s) and allowable design and operational control spanning from elevator to office to terrace. The chosen space, at 250 West 57th Street, has three terraces and full light on three sides and partial light on the fourth.

Once again, simple materials and low partitions were essential to the design. Workstation partitions were topped with custom-designed ceramic planters for added privacy and nature connectedness. These planters were not ready at move in, and the employees noted how much better the space felt once the planters were fully installed.

The design for the space created an axial prospect view across the width of the office that terminates on the planted terraces. Two of the terraces were enhanced with extensive landscaping — the western terrace with a variety of seating and meeting areas and stunning sunset views, and the eastern terrace with food-producing plants, apiaries and an elevated seating area. Maintenance of the Certified Wildlife Habitat® is done by groups of volunteers, which has fostered more interaction among project teams. Employees report that this level of engagement has also strengthened the environmental awareness of a company that has long been a proponent of green design.

FIGURE 7.4 COOKFOX ARCHITECTS, 57TH STREET, NEW YORK CITY, USA, 2017. The COOKFOX studio office has several multifunctional features that make the biophilic space so beloved: (a) a kitchen area with adjacent nooks and a farmhouse table to encourage employees to eat together and away from their computers; (b) work pods with ample potted plants as visual buffer; (c) an elevated corner meeting space with views across the studio, out to the terrace and the city; and (d) a terrace designed to provide quality views from interior offices, outdoor work and event space, vegetable and herb gardens, a protected pollinator habitat and an apiary. A favourite pastime of COOKFOX employees is to go out to the west terrace to watch the sunset over the Hudson River.

Learning from the experience in the prior space, this LEED Platinum and WELL Gold certified office retained excellent prospect and daylight and boasts a variety of indoor and outdoor refuge spaces. From the several conference rooms, to an open booth in the community kitchen, several small phonebooth style rooms and a meditation/mothers' room.

Since completion in 2017, the COOKFOX studio has become a destination for educating clients, students and other visitors on biophilic design and the workplace experience.

CASE STUDY 7.3:
CHANGING THE PERCEPTION OF A SPACE

FIGURE 7.5 PERKINS & WILL, ASID HEADQUARTERS, WASHINGTON, DC, USA, 2016. The shifting wall and ceiling planes create an effective progression into the office, while perceptions of mystery and water, the latter by way of nature-inspired carpet design, infer flow and movement.

A strong advocate for biophilic design, the American Society of Interior Designers (ASID) wanted to create a new headquarters that would be an effective demonstration for their members. The ASID staff tasked their real estate broker with finding a space in Washington, DC that had good access to light on at least two sides.

The downtown location selected was a long and linear space. The Perkins & Will design team used a series of shifted planes and partially revealed views to create a mystery condition that makes the 743m² (8,000ft²) space seem larger. Planter boxes along the windows, including herbs and other plants, create a visual buffer to the urban views. The best views in the entire office have been democratised as a shared corner seating area and library rather than a private office. A super graphic of water ripples extends along the back wall of three adjoining offices. Empurpled and scaled up, the image is abstracted to a point at which it becomes a piece of art.

Completed in 2016, the new headquarters space features human-centric design elements. It was the first space to achieve both a LEED Platinum and a WELL Platinum certification.

Wanting to understand the potential benefits gained by the design of their new space, ASID conducted extensive pre- and post-occupancy studies with their employees. The measurements demonstrated decreases in absenteeism (19%) and self-reported presenteeism (16%) and increases in place attachment (69%) and overall productivity (16%). Just in the first year of occupancy, these improvements were worth £562,693 (US$649,000).[16]

CASE STUDY 7.4:
REDISCOVERING BIOPHILIA IN THE DESIGN PROCESS

In a convergence of live–work–travel, the repositioning of a residential building in downtown Manhattan into a collaborative workplace and hotel began as a journey of discovery for the client and design team. Rodrigo Niño founded The Assemblage to provide 'coworking, co-living, social spaces and natural habitats'; he had realised that crowdfunding for big ideas needed a brick and mortar place for people to assemble. Meyer Davis Studio used this desire for 'physical connectedness' to guide their development of a new workplace design concept that would bring people together in a way that hadn't been experienced elsewhere.

Experientially, the space needed to feel as if to be in it was to step away from the city. Programmatically, the space had to enable coworking, meetings and events with diverse needs, yet remain a welcoming and familiar space. Rooms needed to stay active and capable of being transformed. Blending together programmatic demands and desired experiential outcomes, a concept emerged for the innovation and evolution of both workplace and hospitality — not solely one or the other.

While the completed project is replete with bespoke biophilic interventions, adhering to a biophilic approach was actively avoided in the beginning of the design process for fear of it being a default response to the design problem. The design team felt there needed to be deeper rationale and confidence in using a biophilic lens — that it was the right approach — before broaching the topic with the client.

During the design process, mental health and wellness were identified as priorities. Discussions about materiality and experiential goals led to the decision that the tactile environment needed to foster social and workplace connectedness, as well as connectedness to the earth.

FIGURE 7.6A MEYER DAVIS STUDIO, COMMUNAL MEETING ROOM, THE ASSEMBLAGE JOHN STREET, NEW YORK CITY, USA, 2018. The full wall mural and ample daylight set the tone of the casual space, which easily converts into a theatre.

Over the course of design iterations, biophilia was rediscovered and embraced as a key conduit for responding to these priorities and solving the design problem.

The final design engages the sensory experience through varied spatial and lighting conditions, furniture and upholstery choices and an elixir bar. An immense variety of seating options offer differing degrees and vantage points for prospect and refuge, nurturing a sense of connectedness while accommodating diverse personalities, preferences and work–live activities. A testament to the success of the design is that a significant proportion of members at The Assemblage are reportedly health–oriented professionals.

FIGURE 7.6B–F MEYER DAVIS STUDIO, THE
ASSEMBLAGE, JOHN STREET, NEW YORK CITY,
USA, 2018. The multi–level coworking hotel
embraces unique visual, olfactory, gustatory,
tactile and spatial experiences in the programming
for its communal areas: (b) light–filled living
room; (c) Ayurvedic dining that balances refuge
characteristics with communal experience; (d)
high–back chairs with warm lighting; (e) hot
desks with task lighting; and (f) Elixir bar with
handcrafted, nature–inspired beverages.

FIGURE 7.7 SOFTLAB, ONE STATE STREET, NEW YORK CITY, USA, 2017. The organic geometry of the crystalline dichroic backdrop to the security desk transforms the expansive lobby through added perceptions of dimension, movement and mystery. LEDs cast a range of vivid light that changes in colour, accentuating fragmented reflections of the lobby, as visitors approach. The backlit lantern, balancing the angularity of blocks of ice and ephemeral qualities of stormy clouds, can be seen at night from the street through the floor-to-ceiling glass façade, beckoning passers-by.

FIGURE 7.8 BRIBURN WITH THORNTON TOMASETTI, THE NATURE CONSERVANCY, FORT ANDROSS MILL, BRUNSWICK, MAINE, USA, 2017. To meet project goals — attract talented staff, support workplace well-being and productivity, and inspire innovative and collaborative problem solving — material and visual connections with nature were primary to the biophilic design strategy for this renovation. The curving wood wall with exposed grain made from sustainably harvested yellow birch; the kitchen/lounge countertop crafted from timber salvaged from the bottom of a local river; meeting rooms and workstations that emphasised a balance of privacy, natural light and views to the exterior; and the carpet tile pattern, reminiscent of crashing surf and made from salvaged fishing nets, each contributed to the LEED Gold and WELL certification.

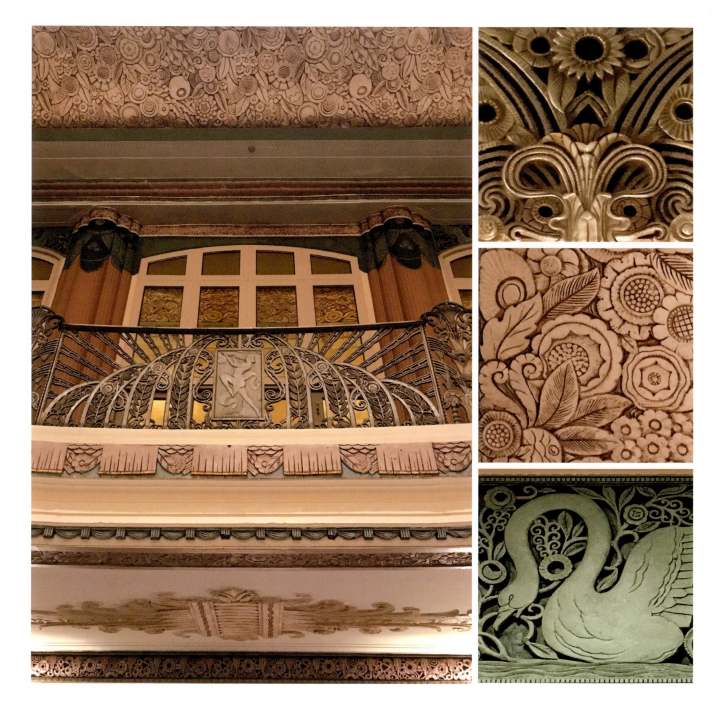

CHAPTER 8

IN THE HOTEL: EXCEPTIONAL GUEST EXPERIENCES

FIGURE 8.1 W. W. AHLSCHLAGER & ASSOCIATES WITH DELANO & ALDRICH, HALL OF MIRRORS, HILTON NETHERLAND PLAZA HOTEL, CAREW TOWER, CINCINNATI, OHIO, USA, 1930. The architectural interior details of this Art Deco building are complex; ornate analogues of nature capture attention and continue to engender awe and appreciation.

HISTORICAL CONTEXT

In the early twentieth century, American architect Mary Colter designed a series of hotels for the Union Pacific railroad. Located across the state of Arizona, each was a masterful celebration of local history and materials, with unique features such as a layered stone fireplace that displayed the strata of rocks that make up the Grand Canyon. The lobby designs created convivial living rooms that encouraged interactions among the travelling guests.

The role of the hotel lobby has since devolved into a transactional space in which guests check in, check out, and perhaps sit and wait briefly for a friend or taxi. In a similar fashion, many hospitality brands have fallen into the trap of having overly fixed design standards that banalises their guest rooms, lobbies and amenity spaces. As brands are discovering the revenue-generating potential of hotel lobbies — where guests and visitors can purchase coffee, wine and food — the old notion of the lobby as the living room for the community is returning. In some models, lobbies have become co-working spaces, available to hotel guests and members of the surrounding community.

Sustainable hospitality has moved in the direction of social resilience. In this respect, locally sourced and fabricated materials, textiles, artworks and amenities, as well as active engagement with the local people and landscape, help to galvanise emotional ties to place and a connection to the economy and cultural heritage of the community.

DESIGN IMPACT OPPORTUNITY

For a biophilic resort or hotel, the lobby, guest rooms, restaurants and bars, spa and wellness facilities and the landscape each offer unique opportunities to introduce or elevate a connection with nature through design. Local culture and philosophies are popular sources of inspiration for biophilic architectural and interior hospitality projects, particularly in boutique hotel design where liberties can be taken with brand aesthetic to achieve a place-based destination.

A balance of visual and material connections with nature and spatial perceptions of prospect (through to other areas of the reception, lobby, amenities), refuge (seating or working nooks) and mystery (winding stairs, perforated partitions) tend to characterise biophilic hotel lobbies. Research has indicated that biophilic lobbies are more likely to increase dwell rate and to positively shape guest perception of a brand.[1]

Biophilic guest rooms are most often characterised by window views, material connections with nature (finishes, headboard, bedding), refuge (canopy bed, window bench, drop ceiling) and dynamic and diffuse light (daylight, task lamps, window blind options, controls). A biophilic strategy accentuates the preferred view. The approach to designing a biophilic guest room should thus differ for rooms with or without scenic views. For rooms without a view, interior finishes and embellishments will be essential to the guest's experience. For rooms with a good view, bed and seating orientations towards the view is an obvious yet notoriously overlooked detail.

Biophilic restaurants and bars are characterised as having successfully integrated natural analogues (finishes, furniture), spatial perceptions of prospect and refuge (elevated booth seats) and multisensory stimuli originating from the culture and cuisine of the place.

In addition to the obvious presence of water, biophilic spa and wellness centres are most often characterised by a strong sense of refuge coupled with dynamic and diffuse light, thermal and airflow variability, and natural materials with differing thermal conductance (Figure 8.2). Multisensory stimuli and a visual connection with nature are often supplements to a biophilic spa strategy.

While market segmentation will naturally be a driver of design and investment decisions, biophilic design can be introduced at any level and scale. With any project, success of implementation will depend on leadership commitment.

FIGURE 8.2 FOSTER + PARTNERS, AURIGA SPA ENTRY SEQUENCE, CAPELLA HOTEL SENTOSA, SENTOSA ISLAND, SINGAPORE, 2009. Aimed at supporting the spa's mission of 'marrying simplicity, nature and indulgence', a wall-mounted school of fish adorns the entry sequence of the spa. Walking along the curvilinear path set deep in the resort, guests traverse a water feature and hillside forest with a canyon–like atmosphere. Dramatic lighting along the wall and reflecting off the water transforms the sculpture into a dynamic school of fish, as if under water. This combination of sculpture, water, lighting and spatial characteristics creates a soothing transitional zone.

CASE STUDY 8.1:
REPOSITIONING A BRAND

FIGURE 8.3A JOHN PORTMAN ARCHITECTS, WESTIN PEACHTREE PLAZA HOTEL, PEACHTREE STREET NW, ATLANTA, GEORGIA, USA, 1976. Biophilic elements were used to create engaging smaller spaces within the cavernous lobby.

The internal design team at Starwood Hotels launched an effort to recast the lobbies and public spaces of Westin hotels using biophilic design. The soaring central lobby of the Westin in downtown Atlanta presented a unique challenge. The original John Portman design was a concrete cylinder surrounded by sky-lit multi-storey open space with concrete walls. The team wanted a space that would invite people to dwell and increase activity at the café bar. A series of interventions, large and small, were used. Adjoining the check-in desk are two small green wall installations. At first blush these might seem like an expensive gesture for something that the guests will only see peripherally, but the front desk staff get the benefit in a windowless space.

The large concrete wall of the central elevator core is now adorned with an oversized painting of local magnolias. The immense surrounding space on the ground floor is broken up into many seating clusters. Along the outer wall a series of refuge spaces are created by using wood screens featuring a biomorphic perforation pattern (Figure 8.3a). These measures help make a somewhat overwhelming space feel intimate and lively.

After Marriott International acquired Starwood, David Kepron, Vice President–Global Design Strategies–Premium Distinctive Brands, embarked on an effort to re-envision the Westin brand. Westin is known for their 'Heavenly Bed', and the brand is being repositioned to focus on a wellness theme. Kepron decided to use biophilic design as part of the redesign of the entire prototype guestroom. Kepron explained that 'because of a better understanding of neuro-physiology — the mind-body connection to experiencing space — the design team is working on better ways to create "cognitive handshakes" throughout Westin, designing rooms and public spaces that respond to an individual's neuro-biological needs'.[2]

Strategies included using wood and natural materials on wall surfaces adjacent to the bed to create a refuge experience reflective materials from the local ecology of each hotel location. Creating a variety of lighting conditions was another focus, including diffused light between the bathroom and bed areas, some circadian lighting and the use of backlit perforated metal panels in the foyer ceiling to create a shadow pattern on the walls and floors similar to the dappled light in a forest (Figure 8.3b).

FIGURE 8.3B MARRIOTT GLOBAL DESIGN
STRATEGIES, PROTOTYPE ROOM, WESTIN, 2018.
The new Westin room prototype supports the
rebranding as a wellness–focused hotel, including
the use of statistical fractals in the design of the
illuminated ceiling plain that casts shadows,
creating an experience of diffused and dappled
light as though walking in a forest.

CASE STUDY 8.2:
A COMPREHENSIVE BIOPHILIC EFFORT

FIGURE 8.4 WOHA, PARKROYAL ON PICKERING, SINGAPORE, 2013. Extensive use of wood in a three-dimensional biomorphic form helps to define the lobby reception and bar while creating a warm welcome in an expansive volume.

Although well known for its verdant terraces and conspicuous fusion of nature and architecture, it is the comprehensive and multidimensional connection with nature that makes the PARKROYAL on Pickering, Singapore, such a beloved example of biophilic design. Through careful evaluation of place, the design team at WOHA used inspiration from the adjacent Hong Lim Park to blur the boundary between outside and inside, creating a concept uniquely reflective of Singaporean culture and ecology.

The main lobby floor — with reception, seating areas, bar and restaurant — is sculpted to connect occupants to the outdoors. Water features flow under foot, plantings climb the walls, and biomorphic elements cross from one amenity to another, from indoors to outdoors. High-backed chairs and perforated screens break down the large volume, creating greater intimacy and further encouraging contemplation of vegetation and water. The ceiling plane of the lobby and adjoining motor court is boldly biomorphic in form and scale, leaving patrons awestruck.

The guest rooms — with a subtle, nature-inspired palette of colours and materials — are designed to direct occupants to the preferred view, out of the windows to the cityscape or cantilevered skygardens. Many guest rooms also capitalise on window views from the bathtubs and showers without compromising guest privacy. The variety and complexity of materials, forms and textures minimised the need for artwork, as did the focus on physical connection to nature on and around the site in both the amenity spaces and guest rooms, minimised the need for artwork.

Because the design differed substantially from other PARKROYAL hotels, the client opted to rebrand the property as the first PARKROYAL COLLECTION hotel. Its popularity has led to significant increases in the average daily room rates.

CASE STUDY 8.3:
CREATING ENDURING EXPERIENCES

Most spas are marketed as being an oasis of calm, yet in design few truly achieve that experience. The Sasanqua Spa on Kiawah Island, South Carolina, designed by Clodagh Design, delivers on this promise.

The 929m² (10,000ft²) facility overlooks the Low Country salt marshes and Kiawah River. The sunlight on Kiawah Island can transition from soft and hazy to bright and harsh. Rather than fight the intensity and glare with technology, the designers chose to use the architecture to manipulate the light and create a play of light and shadow on the interior that shifts with changing daylight conditions. This dynamic light gives drama to the dark palette of natural materials in a quiet hallway (Figure 8.5a).

The configuration of the treatment rooms celebrates the view to the marsh. However, as with many massage treatments, the guest is often not positioned to enjoy a window view (Figure 8.5b). In response to this experiential limitation, the walls of each massage room — particularly zones within the peripheral view from a reclined or procumbent position — were identified as an intervention opportunity to which the design team specified wood panelling with a visible grain. The effect added texture and soft visual intrigue to surfaces of a massage room that are not typically a focus of the design strategy.

Being located near both a marsh and beach also brings the design challenges that come with salt and sand. Materials were chosen to welcome patina over time. As a result of these careful choices, most of the interior, which is over 18 years old, is still adorned with the original finishes and most of the original fabrics. This is an impressive feat given that, as a rule of thumb, most hospitality spaces need refreshing and renovation every seven years.

FIGURE 8.5A–B CLODAGH DESIGN, CORRIDOR AND TREATMENT ROOM, SASANQUA SPA, KIAWAH ISLAND, SOUTH CAROLINA, USA, 2001. The spa corridor design (a) leverages variable daylight conditions to provide an always changing yet inviting circulation in the spa. The spa treatment room (b) features floor-to-ceiling wood panelling, with warm coloured stain and visible grain which can be experienced when the window to the marsh is out of view.

CASE STUDY 8.4:
TRANSPLANTING CULTURE AND PHILOSOPHY

One of several dining venues in Hong Kong by Le Comptoir, the TRi restaurant delivers a Balinese guest experience in The Pulse Shopping Mall in Repulse Bay.

IBUKU used the Balinese philosophy of Tri Hita Karana — the union and balance of man, nature and divinity — to develop a design concept for the restaurant that would transport guests to Bali. Bali's rich cultural heritage and natural beauty inspired the interior design, using Balinese references for the village (Kampung), the garden (Kebun) and the forest (Hutan) to craft a targeted design concept. The distinct views of water and light and distant mountains of Repulse Bay influenced how the architects designed to celebrate naturally occurring changes in experience over the course of the day.

The humble, community-oriented dining area — the Kampung — features woven bamboo panels and mats, as well as a dark colour palette: a tribute to traditional Balinese village homes and hand–craftsmanship. According to architect I. A. Putu Septy Diantari, the IBUKU design team 'wanted to bring balanced energy to the restaurant space. The Kampung bar area is designed as a bale pavilion, a place where Balinese people gather and sit together to relax; our hope was to foster this sense of connection and harmony for TRi'.[3]

The Kebun, or family garden dining section, is expressed as a natural but cultivated area. Patterning from the hollows of sliced bamboo partitions bring about an energising play of light and shadow (Figure 8.6a). A 14.5m long teak log communal table extends the length of the windows.

FIGURE 8.6A IBUKU, PRIVATE DINING AREA,
LE COMPTOIR TRI RESTAURANT, REPULSE BAY,
HONG KONG, 2015. The Kebun dining area is
dominated by natural analogues and a complex
arrangement of bamboo materials, textures
and patterns.

b

FIGURE 8.6B–C IBUKU, HUTAN DINING,
LE COMPTOIR TRI RESTAURANT, REPULSE BAY,
HONG KONG, 2015. The Hutan dining area is
dominated by spatial characteristics emphasising
prospect views, refuge seating and a perception of
risk. Stepping stones leading to pods on the water
create intimate seating for romantic dinners
and for small groups. The oversized lotus-form
seating areas dominate the pond, while becoming
another layer of the view, their silhouettes
echoing the mountain range beyond.

The third dining area captures the wild yet intimate experience of Bali
with strong use of spatial biophilic patterns (Figure 8.6c). The designer
uses rippling water, terracing, cascading ferns and bamboo groves to
transport diners to the Balinese Hutan. Stone table tops made from sliced
river boulders with weathered crusts add dimension and tactile delight to
the dining experience. TRi's materials and hardware palette was infused
with Balinese metalwork, stone and traditional cloth, but bamboo was the
dominant material. 'In relation to the Tri Hita Karana concept', notes IBUKU
Interior Architect Putri Wiwoho, 'bamboo was such a natural choice',[4] not
only for being a sustainable material, but also for having spiritual value.

While the design palette for each of these three spaces had many of the same
attributes, the emphasis on material and spatial characteristics changed from
one space to another, resulting in three entirely different yet unified biophilic
experiences of Balinese culture.

CHAPTER 9

IN THE HOSPITAL: EFFECTIVE HEALING ENVIRONMENTS

FIGURE 9.1 HUBERT WILLIAM HORSLEY, HEATHERWOOD HOSPITAL, ASCOT, BERKSHIRE, UK, 1921. When the estate was first converted to a children's hospital in the early 1920s, ward blocks each had folding doors that opened to a sun terrace onto which patient beds were rolled for a dose of sunlight, fresh air and better views of the outdoors.

HISTORICAL CONTEXT

The Royal Naval Hospital Stonehouse (now a gated residential community known as 'The Millfields') was built by Alexander Rovehead in Plymouth between 1758 and 1765. Rovehead fashioned the hospital as multiple detached wards arranged around a courtyard for the purpose of maximising natural ventilation and minimising the spread of infection. This design was progressive and influential for its time and foreshadowed the 'pavilion' style hospital buildings adopted across Europe and the Colonial Americas.

St. Elizabeth's Hospital, built in 1855 on a hillside overlooking the Potomac River in Washington, DC took these concepts further to incorporate the philosophy that sunlight, fresh air and connection to nature were essential for healing the mentally ill. The wards were laid out in wings that faced gardens and the river and featured large operable windows. Part of the treatment process involved the patients working in vegetable gardens on the grounds. Much of the design and treatment strategy was based on the theories of American physician, Thomas Story Kirkbride, that working in the gardens and seeing plants grow was an important part of the healing process.[1]

In the nineteenth century, Florence Nightingale continued to popularise the pavilion style in her campaign to shift the image of hospitals from being places where the sick go to die, to being places where they go to recuperate and heal. A twentieth century example of this pattern is Heatherwood Hospital in Berkshire (Figure 9.1).

DESIGN IMPACT OPPORTUNITY

Among the most common sources of stress caused by a hospital's environmental conditions are poor control of lighting conditions, noise and confinement in a completely artificial environment.[2] For patients, a stressed body heals more slowly, is less resistant to infection and can experience heightened emotional sensitivity. For nurses, being in suboptimal health increases the likelihood of making medical errors.[3]

Roger Ulrich's 1984 study[4] of the benefits of a view to nature from a hospital bed is largely credited for underpinning much of the adoption of healing gardens in medical facilities. Beyond the benefits of improved patient outcomes, documented decreases in occupational stress among staff has been significant.[5] The healing gardens now found in many hospitals around the world are typically oriented as a centrally accessible space enjoyed by patients and staff alike.

Healing gardens and controlled access to daylight — being the most researched biophilic characteristics in healthcare — are primary design opportunities for achieving measurably improved health outcomes. Decreased boredom, reduced duration of hospital stays, lowered consumption of pain medications, and fewer negative evaluative comments from nurses are among the research–based design opportunities,[6 7 8 9 10] as is decreased stress and increased workplace satisfaction among staff,[11] and improved visitor experience for family members and visitors.[12]

FIGURE 9.2 RMJM ARCHITECTS AND CPG ARCHITECTS, KHOO TECK PUAT HOSPITAL, YISHUN CENTRAL, SINGAPORE, 2010. As one component of a holistic vision for healing and well-being, the community gardens on the roof of the clinical wing are visible from many of the patient wards. The gardens are part of the hospital administrator's philosophy that healing, health and well-being are a community function, not to be hidden away.

CASE STUDY 9.1:
HEALING GARDENS, INSIDE OUT

FIGURE 9.3 HOK AND CPG ARCHITECTS, NG TENG FONG GENERAL HOSPITAL, JURONG, SINGAPORE, 2015. The design strategy focused on bringing a view of nature to every bed in the hospital. This was achieved by having vertical windows by the head of each bed looking out onto small tropical gardens that stair step up the building.

CPG and HOK, the designers for Ng Teng Fong General Hospital in Singapore, took a decentralised approach to healing gardens by bringing the garden to the patient's bed. Ng Teng Fong is a public hospital, part of the Singapore national healthcare system and, as such, common wards are not air conditioned. To ensure good cross-ventilation the wards are on single-sided corridors. Each ward houses four to six beds arranged in a fan-shaped pattern. Adjacent to the head of each bed is a floor-to-ceiling operable window looking out onto a small sky garden (Figure 9.3). These gardens of palms and other tropical plantings stair step up the façade looking. This arrangement ensures that every bed, even when curtains between beds are drawn, always has a view to the vegetation outside. Lip Chuan of CPG Architects said that with a natural ventilation strategy it was crucial to design a louvre venting system that brings in air effectively when the windows are closed during monsoon rains.

Nursing stations are typically located at corridor intersections and may have small adjacent planted areas and access to daylight as well. In some areas, because real wood cannot be used on hospital floors, tiles that mimic wood planks and flooring that has flower patterns are used to make additional connections to nature. A water garden is located near a break area for employees on one of the roof areas, and can also be viewed from many patient rooms.

CASE STUDY 9.2:
CHANGING THE PATIENT EXPERIENCE

FIGURE 9.4A CANNON DESIGN, PATIENT ROOM, JACOBS MEDICAL CENTER, UNIVERSITY OF CALIFORNIA SAN DIEGO, LA JOLLA, CALIFORNIA, USA, 2016. Changing the orientation of the bed and expanding the view from the bed, while removing acoustic and visual clutter, dramatically improves the patient experience.

The presence of modern medical equipment can often dominate the experience of a hospital room. The visual clutter and noise can make it difficult for patients to relax, sleep and heal, and can exacerbate feelings of vulnerability. The typical patient room configuration positions the bed perpendicular to the wall with the head of the bed surrounded by equipment and connections, sometimes obstructing the view out of the window.

For the design of the Jacobs Medical Center at the University of California, San Diego, Cannon Design's Mehrdad Yazdani wanted to re-envision the layout of the prototypical patient room. His team was challenged with how the design of the room could contribute to a better patient experience — whether the view could be directly visible; how best to diminish the overwhelming presence of monitors and other equipment; and whether patients could be given a better sense of control.

The result was a patient room with the head of the bed placed in a wedge-shaped headwall, which offered a refuge condition and hid a majority of the equipment and connections (Figure 9.4a). The angular positioning of the bed meant that the window view was clearly visible, without the patient having to turn their head, while keeping their face visible to nursing staff looking through the door.

The room was given a hospitality design feel, with a window sill that started at the floor, faux wood wall finishes for their calming effect and comfortable seating for visitors. Patients could remotely operate the window shades, which increased their sense of control and reduced the number of nursing calls. The combination of surface materials, room angles, controls for patients and careful equipment placement also led to substantially less noise disturbance compared to the adjoining older facility.

FIGURE 9.4B CANNON DESIGN, SERENITY ROOM, JACOBS MEDICAL CENTER, UNIVERSITY OF CALIFORNIA SAN DIEGO, LA JOLLA, CALIFORNIA, USA, 2016. As part of the Center's chaplain services and spiritual care programme, the Serenity Room, with its soft light, woodgrain pews and curved edges, offers a non–threatening and meditative space for patients, visitors and staff alike.

The design grew out of a highly collaborative process involving 65 user groups, 80 hospital departments and 513 user meetings.[13] Architect Nadine Quirmbach said that the team had to fight for a number of biophilic elements. They worked with a manufacturer to prove the bed canopy assembly would be durable and that the wedge–shaped room would not impede movement of patient beds in and out of the rooms. They also had to overcome concerns that having visible woodgrain finish on the wall unit would confuse patients on heavy medication. The floor–to–ceiling glazing and motorised shades were more expensive design options, but the designers were able to convince the hospital that they were crucial to the patient experience.

The extensive windows and daylight have made wayfinding easier for patients and visitors. The abundant access to daylight has positively changed the nurses' attitudes. The medical centre's conference facility and chapel (Figure 9.4b) featuring biomorphic forms, wood finishes and dramatic lighting have been very popular. Nadine emphasised that the additional time needed to ensure these features survived the design process was worth the effort, particularly because newer hospital designs have since been clearly inspired by Cannon's work at Jacobs.

CASE STUDY 9.3:
CREATING A SAFE AND SUPPORTIVE SPACE

Maggie's Yorkshire is a centre for cancer patients undergoing treatment at St. James's University Hospital in Leeds, UK. Heatherwick Studio designed the 480m² (5,166ft2) facility to fit on a steeply-sloped infill site on the medical campus. To restore the green space that had been on the site, their design strategy was to create a building that is, in effect, a series of stepping giant planters that lift the garden onto the roof. The spaces between the planters are shared and social while the interiors of each planter are quiet, private spaces. The structural system to support the outer rims of each planter is a radius of cantilevered wood arms, that together create a tree-like composition. This produces a series of interior spaces that could be described as being within a forest, with views out to clearings.

One of the central challenges was to create an institutional facility capable of handling 30,000 patients a year, while still feeling intimate and residential. The solution needed to be intentionally simple but complex at the same time, starting with the exclusion of a reception desk, one that would ordinarily be situated at the entry for intercepting patients coming from the oncology centre to the entrance of Maggie's. Instead, patients are greeted by an embracing and residential entry with apparent wayfinding and glimpses of adjacent rooms (Figure 9.5).

Four biophilic patterns — Biomorphic Forms, Dynamic and Diffuse Light, Material Connection with Nature and Mystery — were primary to the design. A mystery condition was intentional in the space planning sequence; all of the public spaces needed to be readily visible from the entrance area; unique spatial conditions were designed to bring in daylight in obscure ways; and each view through one interior space was designed to offer just enough information to pull visitors into the next space. Materials

FIGURE 9.5 HEATHERWICK STUDIO, MAGGIE'S YORKSHIRE, ST JAMES'S UNIVERSITY HOSPITAL. LEEDS, UK, 2020. Millwork, textures and lighting are at the heart of the biophilic experience at Maggie's. The tree canopy archways of the reception create a welcoming and embracing refuge–like residential experience.

were selected that could be easily repaired and that would visibly age and patina in ways that would give the space a feeling of being cherished.

In stark but welcoming contrast to the medical campus in which Maggie's is nestled, the ribbed canopy of the interior is mirrored on the exterior as a tiered structure adorned with vegetation and flowers — communicating a message of life and abundance.

CASE STUDY 9.4:
BENEFITTING STAFF AND PATIENTS

FIGURE 9.6A ORGA ARCHITECT, MONDZORG MIDDENMEER DENTAL CLINIC, MIDDENMEER, THE NETHERLANDS, 2014. Treatment rooms are arrayed toward the savannahh landscape, away from a road, offering patients and staff a continuous view to nature, as well as the curiously novel bird perched atop the door frame.

The Mondzorg Middenmeer dental practice designed by Daan Bruggink of ORGA architect is a small, single-storey facility in a suburban setting. The dentist had read about healing environments and was interested in a building that would support both patients and staff. The site was surrounded by trees and had views onto a meadow, making it a great setting for direct visual connections to nature. A curvilinear layout allowed for a series of treatment rooms (Figure 9.6a) and a circulation spine with floor-to-ceiling windows (Figure 9.6b) which strategically maximised the views.

In explaining the design process and outcomes, Bruggink said that 'when seated in the dentist's chair, patients can indeed look out across the (very flat) Dutch landscape. This was actually one of our design principles: letting the patient experience the long range view, the weather and the natural surroundings from the treatment rooms. The window frames to the corridor and to the outside have been positioned specifically for this purpose. This affects the dentists and assistants sitting next to the chairs as well . They also profit from this connection to the natural surroundings during their work hours'.[14]

Exterior conditions (Figure 9.6c) were leveraged to support a serene interior experience. The treatment rooms look to nature through the corridor, which could leave the patients feeling exposed to people passing by en route to other treatment rooms. To address patient privacy, the treatment room windows have a film that allows views out, but not into the rooms. In addition to extensive daylighting and ample views to nature, the building has an exposed wood structure. Painted on the interior walls are life-sized renderings of local birds and animals to be discovered (Figures 9.6a and 9.6b), particularly by children, when moving through the building and treatment rooms.

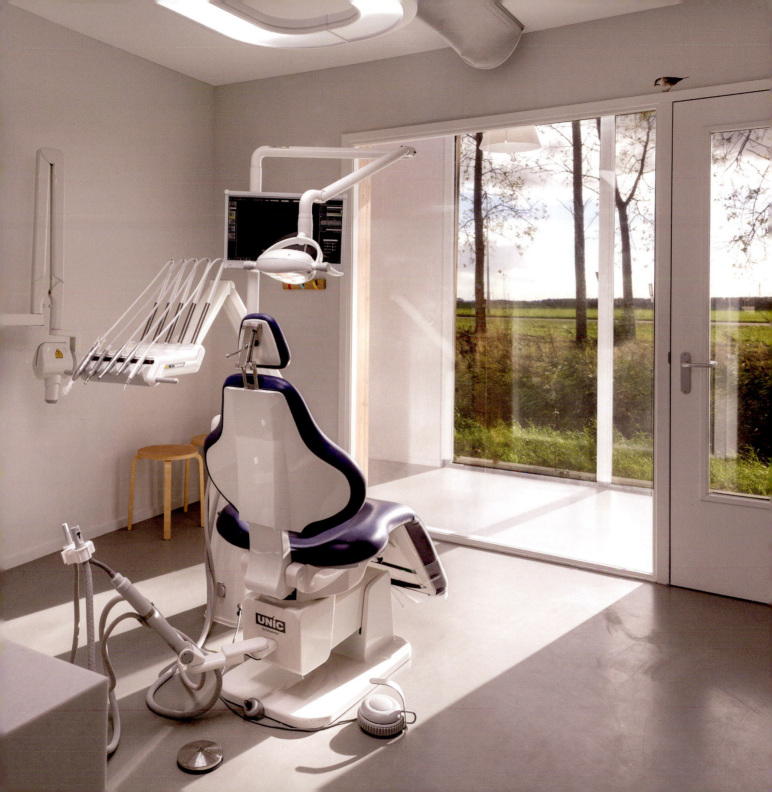

FIGURE 9.6B–C ORGA ARCHITECT, MONDZORG MIDDENMEER DENTAL CLINIC, MIDDENMEER, THE NETHERLANDS, 2014. (b) A simple materials palette is intended to be calming, with strategically placed, nature-inspired treasures for discovery, like the life-sized fawn at the end of this hallway; (c) a view from the meadow of the exterior and green roof.

CASE STUDY 9.5:
FOSTERING AGENCY AND OUTCOMES

The Emergency Psychiatric Ward at Östra Psychiatric Hospital in Göteberg, Sweden, was designed by White Arkitekter to support the health and well-being needs of the patients and staff. Evidence-based design focus on biophilia, was an important part of the project.

The 1,200m² (12,917ft²) building was completed in 2006, and included several biophilic design strategies to create a calming, restorative space for patients experiencing mental illness. The wards were arranged so that all patient rooms have views to the outside, and so that there could be two internal glazed conservatories. Wayfinding is facilitated by clear prospect views on main circulation corridors, and small internal atrium gardens. There is extensive use of wood in the interiors, and warmly coloured walls. The layout maximises daylight exposure throughout.

Because the project replaced an older facility that served the same number of patients, the team was able to compare a number of results. A pioneering pre- and post-occupancy study of patients at Östra substantiated the connection between physical environment and patient health. There were significant reductions in violent episodes, compulsory injections and readmission after seven days. There was also evidence of reduced recovery time for depression patients. Furthermore, staff sick listing decreased from 9% to 6% following the redesign.[15]

FIGURE 9.7 WHITE ARKITEKTER, ÖSTRA
PSYCHIATRIC HOSPITAL, GÖTEBERG, SWEDEN,
2006. Brightly day-lit corridors support
wayfinding and reduce stress, and an interior
glazed solarium offers respite while encouraging
unescorted independence.

IN THE FACTORY:
PRODUCTIVE MANUFACTORIES

FIGURE 10.1 THOMAS WORTHINGTON & SONS,
DENTAL HOSPITAL, MANCHESTER UNIVERSITY,
UK, 1940. The high-quality daylight coming
through the large windows of this mechanical
laboratory enabled focused and detailed work
without electric lighting. Views out of the
windows also help to prevent visual fatigue.

HISTORICAL CONTEXT

For more than 80 years, business students have been taught the 'Hawthorne effect', which purports that physical changes (e.g. lighting levels) made in the work environment were a signal of management's concern for the workers. The study concluded that the characteristics of the workspace itself were not indicators of productivity and that the attentiveness of management was the primary factor leading to increased outputs.[1]

According to Dutch psychologist Michiel Kompier,[2] the proliferation of supposed lessons from the Great Depression–era Hawthorne study represented 'a major historical event in the development of social sciences'. He has also noted that 'in industrial sociology or psychology, no other theory or set of experiments has stimulated more research and controversy nor contributed more to a change in management thinking than the Hawthorne studies and the human relations movement they spawned'.

It is now known that the Hawthorne research was deeply flawed and statistically insignificant,[3][4] yet the case study is still taught in business schools today, without mention of myths having been debunked in the 1970s.

In addition, since the advent of accessible electric lighting (coincidentally around the same time as the Hawthorne research), sterility and protection of intellectual property have been drivers of factory design and, until recently, precluded most biophilic design interventions.

Dependency on electric lighting has the devaluation of the workplace — omitting windows — and the devaluation of the human experience. Factory design has forgotten that daylight is both free and good for the occupant's health and performance; that views to moving trees, grasses and wildlife are good for eye health and mental stimulation; and that views of the sky and to other people are instrumental to perceiving the passage of time. These experiences can be designed back in.

DESIGN IMPACT OPPORTUNITY

In a production area, aside from workplace safety, the needs of machines and equipment in a production area often take precedence over the needs of the people who operate the equipment. Designing for the human experience of each space type can be just as important as finding the perfect balance of office, communal, meeting, lab and production space types. For any space with full-time equivalent occupancy (i.e. more than four consecutive hours per day), the physical environment and experience of that space becomes essential to maintaining occupant health and well-being.

Bringing daylight into the space can increase productivity through improvements in visual acuity that can reduce defects and production rates.[5] Reducing stress and improving cognitive performance are desired outcomes that can be achieved through the integration of nature and natural patterns. In accordance with attention restoration theory, bringing experiences of nature into a factory, bakery or laboratory should lead to gains in productivity. Given the limitations of bringing live plants into manufacturing settings, the strategies that seem to be most effective are views to the outside, representational nature inside and break spaces that support refuge and other connections with nature.

CASE STUDY 10.1:
RETHINKING THE WINDOWLESS BOX

FIGURE 10.2 WILLIAM MCDONOUGH, HERMAN MILLER GREENHOUSE, HOLLAND, MICHIGAN, USA, 1995. At the Greenhouse, visual access to daylight and nature views have increased psychological and social well-being, as well as productivity.

Herman Miller is well established as a manufacturer of office furniture. In the mid-1990s the company was preparing to move 700 employees from a large windowless factory into a new building, the Herman Miller Greenhouse (Figure 10.2), designed by William McDonough. The new building was designed to have a fully daylit interior, utilising numerous clerestory skylights and windows with views out into a restored native prairie landscape and water features. The roughly 2,740m^2 (295,000ft^2) facility was arranged with offices, meeting spaces and entrances to the manufacturing floor along the outer edge of the curving façade. The conditions inside the factory were consistent, with bright light, day and night.

The US Department of Energy sponsored a year-long study to see if this new green building would result in a gain in productivity by company employees. Upon initial analysis, the data showed there was a 'total quality management' score increase of approximately 2%. This was good result; however, when fully aggregated, the performance data appeared incongruous. Once the data was sorted by work shifts, the differences became clear; the night shift did not show significant gains in productivity, the swing shift showed mixed data, and the daytime shift showed significant gains in productivity. In experiential terms, the daytime shift received the benefit of the view to the surrounding landscape that the other shifts lacked.[67]

The Herman Miller Greenhouse facility continues to be a precedent for how coordination of interior, architectural and landscape design can enhance the physical and mental health of building occupants, as well as corporate productivity and profits to boot.

CASE STUDY 10.2:
EXPRESSING THE COMPANY ETHOS

FIGURE 10.3A TERRAPIN BRIGHT GREEN,
BIOPHILIC INTERVENTION MAP, CLIF BAR
BAKERY, TWIN FALLS, IDAHO, USA, 2016.
Biophilic design interventions were mapped out
in the plan review for the public and non-sterile
staff areas of the bakery.

The inherently sterile interior of an industrial bakery would seem an unlikely candidate for biophilic design. Clif Bar, a nutrition bar manufacturer catering to outdoor athletes, has strong sustainability goals. Their headquarters office in Emeryville, California, is located in an old daylit warehouse constructed of old-growth redwood. The building has a variety of spatial experiences and courtyard gardens, great access to daylight, and makes extensive use of natural materials. Their nutrition bars were baked by several co-packing companies. When Clif Bar decided to build their own bakery in Twin Falls, Idaho, the design challenge was to build a facility that reflected their outdoor ethic and made a strong tie to nature for their employees.

An industrial bakery is an over 300m (1,000ft) long space that must be kept sterile. Natural materials, plants, even artwork that might collect dust and harbour microbial growth, are prohibited. Windows and skylights can be problematic for both condensation issues and potential industrial espionage. The facility would be located in a former farm field near a huge windowless yogurt factory. The design team was tasked with translating the feeling of the Emeryville office space to the Twin Falls bakery.

The design team chose to concentrate a variety of biophilic experiences in the entrance, public and non-sterile staff areas of the building (Figure 10.3a). The main circulation corridor has a feature wall that uses local stone to reference the nearby canyon where the Twin Falls are located. Rough finished wood is used in a number of applications. The main break room and cafeteria has extensive windows onto the surrounding landscape near and far. There are a variety of seating choices, including booths along the back wall and a cluster of high-backed seating nooks. There is a small garden in an internal courtyard near the main event space, and plantings in the office and other areas. The priority was to include many biophilic elements for associates to experience during break periods and at the beginning or end of a shift.

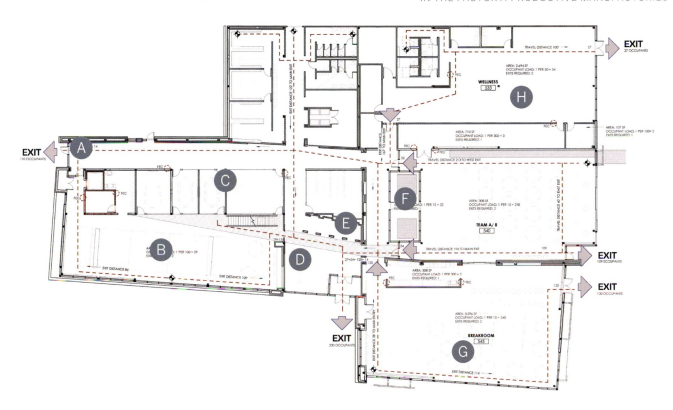

MARKER	PROGRAMME	PROPOSED BIOPHILIC INTERVENTION	BIOPHILIC PATTERN REFERENCE
A	Hallway Corridors	Biomorphic art at the terminus of long hallway corridors	Biomorphic Forms and Patterns; Mystery
B	Open Office Area	Refuge areas and ensure that views are unobstructed	Prospect; Refuge
C	Conference Rooms	Natural finishes and install vegetation	Visual Connection with Nature; Material Connection with Nature
D	Reception	Vegetation	Visual Connection with Nature
E	Aspiration Area	Small water feature behind the five aspirations	Presence of Water
F	Atrium	Water feature and native plantings that change seasonally	Presence of Water; Connection with Natural Systems
G	Break Room	Vegetated wall system and refuge area	Visual Connection with Nature; Refuge
H	Wellness Center	Bouldering/belay climbing wall with natural features	Biomorphic Forms and Patterns; Complexity and Order

Within the bakery itself there are high windows along one outer wall. They were designed high enough to prevent people outside the building from being able to view or photograph proprietary industrial equipment, but low enough to allow a view to the sky and, once grown in, to some of the trees planted on the perimeter of the site. These trees are part of a walking/running trail established around the site and through the native plantings in the stormwater swales. There is also an area for an organic garden.

As with the Herman Miller factory (see Case Study 10.1), the windows provide a benefit during the daytime shift, some parts of the year for the swing shift, but no benefit for the night shift. Recognising this limitation, and the imperative to benefit all the associates within the sterile bakery area, a different strategy would be necessary. Based on the knowledge that even a picture of nature has measurable benefit,[8] the team came upon an idea to capitalise on Clif Bar's daily social media feed, which displays photographs of people in nature enjoying their products. The tall white metal walls throughout the interior of the bakery can act as large screens for projecting these images, which can then change on a regular basis. This solution that connects Clif Bar associates both to nature and to the ethos of the company.

FIGURE 10.3B BABCOCK DESIGN, CLIF BAR
BAKERY, TWIN FALLS, IDAHO, USA, 2016. Clif
Bar's culture and ethos are reflected in the wood
and stone materials throughout the corridors and
other non-production areas, through language
and imagery, and through access to the outdoors.

FIGURE 10.4 DNA_DESIGN AND ARCHITECTURE, BROWN SUGAR FACTORY AND COMMUNITY CENTER, LISHUI, CHINA, 2016. During the day workers have a fantastic view to the landscape and community through expansive windows. When lit at night, the etched glass, featuring images of farming sugar cane, creates a sense of enclosure while continuously connecting workers to the landscape.

IN THE COMMUNITY: CONVIVIAL CIVIC SPACES

FIGURE 11.1 EERO SAARINEN WITH HARRY BERTOIA AND THEODORE ROSZAK, MIT CHAPEL, MASSACHUSETTS INSTITUTE OF TECHNOLOGY, CAMBRIDGE, MASSACHUSETTS, USA, 1956. Sunlight glitters off the metal pieces of Bertoia's sculpture over the marble altar in Saarinen's MIT Chapel. The surrounding scalloped brick walls are animated by the reflections of water rippling in the basin that continue to inspire awe more than 60 years after being built.

HISTORICAL CONTEXT

The *res publica*, or the civic body of a community, needs places in which the interactions that support a public life can occur. Some of these are the 'third places',[1] where daily interactions happen on both a small and grand scale, while others are places of refuge or study within the public realm. Roman, Turkish and Japanese bath houses were part of their communities' civitas. Post offices and public libraries are contemporary examples. The spaces can be grand or intimate, but all support civic interaction.

DESIGN IMPACT OPPORTUNITY

Because the formation of community in the 21st century is frequently online and spatially distant virtual networks, the need to support place-based community is even more important. By designing spaces that 'reflect and respond to local geography... support direct interaction with nature...', as described in the Center for Active Design's Civic Guidelines,[2] biophilic design can focus on celebrating natural assets unique to a site to help boost civic trust and community pride.

To be truly effective civic spaces, equitable access is essential. This is more than just physical access improvements to transportation systems. The spaces themselves must be usable by people of differing abilities, cultures and sensitivities, yet designed for the local context of place and community. This is where biophilic design can help to elevate effective civic spaces beyond the inclusion of vegetation.

The incorporation of biophilic spatial patterns — particularly prospect, refuge, awe — is a fairly universal design essential for achieving meaningful biophilic experience in libraries, transit hubs, places of worship and other civic spaces.

Prospect is a classic characteristic of civic spaces, particularly of town centres and historic transit hubs. Even civic provisions of refuge, such as covered public seating areas, offer strong prospect.

Spaces that are designed to induce a sense of awe can subsequently encourage prosocial behaviours.[3] Civic spaces can be designed to impose the power of the state over the individual — which can engender humiliation, rather than humility — or they can be designed to create a sense of charitability and convivial behaviour. Biophilic characteristics of awe support the latter outcome.

Biophilic places of worship almost always balance dynamic and diffuse light, prospect and awe (Figure 11.2). Many also successfully incorporate complexity and order, biomorphic forms and other natural analogues.

Good civic spaces also support casual interaction at a variety of levels depending on an individual's state of mind. Public lobbies and airport lounges are prime examples; some are open, with seating that encourages interaction, while others offer more reclusive seating pods from which to observe but not necessarily engage.

Public libraries have moved beyond being solely repositories for books. In many communities they also provide spaces for community meetings, entrepreneurial start-ups and media production. More importantly, the library is frequently the one non-commercial building in a community where the public can gather and interact.

FIGURE 11.2 YUSEF ABDELKI OF HALCROW GROUP, SHEIKH ZAYED GRAND MOSQUE, ABU DHABI, UAE, 2007. As in many mosques, this interior design supports an interplay of organic and fractal patterned surfaces with dynamic and diffuse light in a volume that provides a profound sense of prospect and awe.

CASE STUDY 11.1:
CONTEMPLATING COMMUNITY MENTAL HEALTH

The Windhover Contemplative Center is a 371.6m² (4,000ft²) public gallery on the campus of Stanford University in Northern California. Aidlin Darling Design created a space to exhibit five of Nathan Oliveira's paintings inspired by kestrels swooping above the Stanford foothills (Figure 11.3a). The main patrons commissioned the building with the intention that it would pair art and nature to help facilitate contemplation, seeing it as a way to 'recentre oneself'.

According to the architect, Joshua Aidlin, a campus study of student mental health issues led the team to realise that the task was not just to design a building for art, but to help the community regain health, balance and wellness.

From the beginning, students, staff and faculty were consulted for the design. Aidlin noted that 'Students wanted to use the space. We met with them early on and talked to them about their needs. Everyone has different paterns for when they are stressed out. Undergrads have different views than graduates.' Based on these differing needs, the final design offered multiple spaces and pathways for contemplation and reflection.

The interlocking processional spaces (Figure 11.3b) take the visitors through a series of three stereometric refuges, each interrupted by two open-air courtyards (Figure 11.3c). These two space types play off one another: one has extensive views out across the landscape, while the other has indirect and diffuse lighting with opaque rammed earth walls and slivers of distant landscaping between 15 and 30m (50 and 100ft) away. Benches are positioned in relation to views and artwork.

Almost all surfaces were composed of materials and elements from nature that, through minimal processing, reflect the local ecology and geology to create a distinct sense of place. Aidlin notes, 'It was critical to Nathan Oliveira that the space feel organic, not like a stark white museum'.

FIGURE 11.3A AIDLIN DARLING DESIGN,
WINDHOVER CONTEMPLATIVE CENTER,
STANFORD UNIVERSITY, CALIFORNIA, USA,
2014. Nathan Oliveira's monumental paintings set
the tone for the building and were the inspiration
for creating a series of reflective spaces.

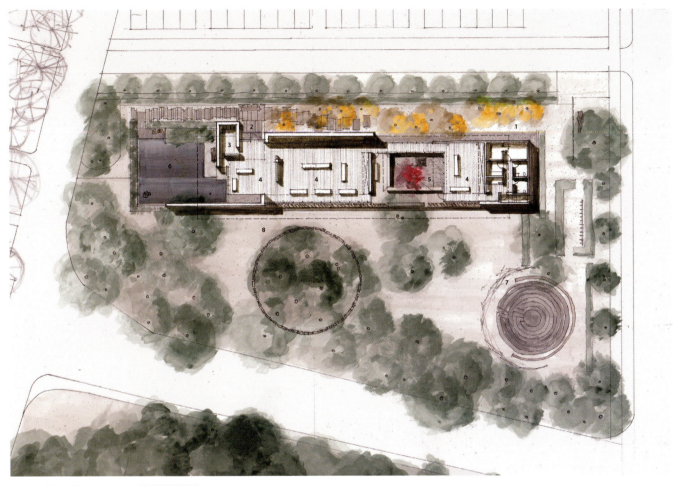

1 ENTRY GARDEN
2 ENTRY
3 INFORMATION VESTIBULE
4 GALLERY
5 EXTERIOR COURTYARD
6 REFLECTING POOL
7 MEDITATION LABYRINTH
8 CONTEMPLATIVE GROVE

0' 5' 10'   20'

b

FIGURE 11.3B–C AIDLIN DARLING DESIGN,
WINDHOVER CONTEMPLATIVE CENTER,
STANFORD UNIVERSITY, CALIFORNIA, USA,
2014. (b) The site plan shows how spaces are
visually connected as one, while (c) the interior
courtyards offer unique experiences, degrees of
refuge, and proximity to nature.

CASE STUDY 11.2:
EVOLVING THE DESIGN PROCESS

FIGURE 11.4 SHEPLEY BULFINCH, PHIPPS CONSERVATORY AND BOTANICAL GARDENS, PITTSBURGH, PENNSYLVANIA, USA. For the three projects at Phipps, (a) biophilic design workshops were repeatedly used throughout the design process; (b) documentation of workshops and certifications helped to identify opportunities for improvements; (c) some biophilic interventions were simple and artistic; and (d) other biophilic interventions focused on the experience of the landscape and building together.

First built in 1893 as a Victorian-style greenhouse designed by Lord & Burnham, the Phipps Conservatory and Botanical Gardens in Pittsburgh has evolved from being a facility to display exotic plants to a centre for environmental education. In addition to its many accolades for sustainable and energy-efficient design, Phipps has had the foresight to evolve its approach to biophilic design over the course of three development projects, each one introducing biophilic design at a different intervention point.

The first project was the Center for Sustainable Landscapes, a building that achieved Platinum certifications under the LEED®, WELL® and SITES systems, BREEAM 6 Stars, as well as Living Building Challenge (LBC), which has a notable emphasis on biophilic design. This building was Phipps's introduction to biophilic design. Working with The Design Alliance Architects, views of nature, daylight and natural ventilation were included in the final design.

After project completion, feeling that additional opportunities could still be pursued, the Phipps team explored the use of art. This initiative led to the creation of the BETA (Biophilia Enhanced Through Art) Project which, through workshops between staff and facilitator Sonja Bochart, resulted in a final product that engaged a wide variety of artists and media to greatly improve the biophilic experience inside the building. In the art installation, occupants experience transmitted local nature sounds, not through speakers, but rather through the actual structure and glass façade of the building atrium.

The second project, the Exhibit Staging Center, was also designed to meet LEED Platinum, WELL Platinum and the LBC. Working with FortyEighty Architecture and Shepley Bulfinch, a biophilic design workshop occurred mid–design and significantly helped the design team integrate biophilic design more organically and thoroughly into the project. While pleased with the outcomes, Phipps believed biophilic design could have been even more influential had it been introduced sooner in the project timeline.

For the Nature Lab project, Phipps decided to incorporate biophilic design into the project on day one, making it a major driver for the entire project and all six of the project's integrative design workshops. With this third project, everyone on the design team, from engineers to architects to staff, were fully engaged in creating a meaningful biophilic design experience. As Phipps President and CEO Richard Piacentini explained, 'It changed the conversation we had throughout the design and it shows in the work'.

FIGURE 11.5 TURKISH AIRLINES LOUNGE, ISTANBUL, TURKEY, C. 2018. The biomorphic pavilions divide an expansive lounge into a series of more intimate seating areas. The arches, formed with a fractal pattern similar to classic Turkish tile mosaics, diffuse and distribute light into a decorative patterning that changes over the course of the day.

FIGURE 11.6 PARIS CHARLES DE GAULLE AIRPORT, ROISSY–EN–FRANCE, FRANCE, C. 2018. Biophilic design can be effective in light retrofits like this lounge area in Terminal 2E of the Roissy Airport that uses an abstracted tree light fixture, paired with panelling and comfortable seating, to help create a calming respite.

CASE STUDY 11.3:
DRAWING PEOPLE IN

FIGURE 11.7A SNØHETTA, CALGARY NEW CENTRAL LIBRARY, CALGARY, ALBERTA, CANADA, 2018. The curving atrium lined with Western red cedar creates a mystery condition that draws people up through the building. In the year after opening, the library had 1.7 million visitors, far exceeding estimations.

The new Central Library in Calgary, Canada, is part of a new generation of libraries. While centrally located within the city, the surrounding landscaping is predominantly local native species. The building is wrapped in a metal skin that is perforated with clear and fritted translucent panels that form an abstraction to be interpreted as snowflakes or ice crystals. This creates a dynamic light and shadow pattern within the adjoining spaces. According to Sarah Meilleur, Director of Service Delivery for the Calgary Public Libraries, '... changing light and clouds combine to produce these moments of surprise and delight...', even for people who have been in the spaces multiple times before.[4]

The entry is covered by a curving sloped ceiling of Western red cedar, which then extends into the core. This shape resonates with Calgarians by mimicking Chinook cloud formations that signal warming winds on cold winter days. The shape of the cedar–lined central atrium is reminiscent of a First Nations canoe. Meilleur said that the curving sight lines along the core and stairwell '...draws you up through the building to explore'.[5]

The reading areas have a mixture of open, prospect–dominated spaces paired with more intimate perimeter seating, some with views of artworks created by First Nations artists or out to the river. The main reading room seats 150 people and, while frequently filled, is reportedly always naturally quiet due to the calming effect of the design.

Quotations are engraved in the mullions of the reading room, revealed to occupants only at specific sun angles over the course of the day, reinforcing both the orderliness and information richness of the space.

a

FIGURE 11.7B SNØHETTA, CALGARY NEW CENTRAL LIBRARY, CALGARY, ALBERTA, CANADA, 2018. The combination of skin and glazing materials along with the angled mullions produces a pleasing dynamic lighting experience in the reading areas.

FIGURE 11.8 MECANOO, DELFT CITY HALL AND TRAIN STATION, THE NETHERLANDS, 2015. While the awe-inspiring ceiling in the station's central hall is the main appeal, the subtle biophilic characteristics along the corridors and entry portals are more essential to buffering travellers from the stresses of the urban transit experience. The biomorphic curvatures soften what would otherwise be a very rectilinear space, while walls and columns adorned with familiar blue tiles tie the space to Delft.

CHAPTER 12

IN THE URBAN LANDSCAPE:
RESTORATIVE POCKET PARKS
AND PROMENADES

FIGURE 12.1 CALVERT VAUX AND FREDERICK LAW OLMSTED, OAK BRIDGE, CENTRAL PARK, NEW YORK CITY, USA, 1860. Early articulations of prospect, refuge and visual and physical access to nature for public health and well–being are even more prominent and beloved in these parks 150 years later.

HISTORICAL CONTEXT

In 1843, the Birkenhead Commissioners hired English gardener and architect Joseph Paxton (1803–1865) to design the first publicly funded civic park in the world. Their intent was to create a park to support the well-being of the growing industrial workforce in Birkenhead, Merseyside, England. The site, originally a low marshy area, was rebuilt with lakes, meadows, hills and some buildings;[1] in effect, a restorative countryside landscape. The design had a significant influence on American landscape architect Frederick Law Olmsted (1822–1903) who, in partnership with English architect Calvert Vaux (1824–1895), would go on to design Central Park (Figure 12.1) and Prospect Park in New York City,[2] and influence generations of thinkers and designers about the role of public parks in urban life.

The biophilic characteristics of these early feats in landscape architecture — primarily prospect, refuge, water and a physical connection with nature — have, over the years, been replicated the world over at much smaller urban scales, from promenades to small urban pocket parks to tactical 'urban acupuncture' interventions on the urban fabric.

DESIGN IMPACT OPPORTUNITY

Homes, parks, transportation nodes, commercial spaces and public buildings make up the economic fabric of communities. These and other spatial elements of a community have psychological and physiological impacts on the inhabitants.

An increasingly sedentary, indoor lifestyle has been tied to many of the leading health crises for industrialised countries, including obesity, type II diabetes, high blood pressure, heart disease and certain cancers.[3] The World Health Organization has linked diminished participation in outdoor physical activity to a lack of parks in urbanised areas.[4] Spending time in a park can reduce behavioural symptoms of ADD or ADHD in children.

Greater concentration and attention rates are enabled after walking in the park, leading to reduced medication intake, and thus reduced medical expenses for families.[5]

Environmental factors like tree canopy and parks contribute to the character of a community, increase perceptions of health[6] and affect decisions to engage in physical activity during leisure time. There is a greater willingness to walk when the route is believed to include more natural features.[7] Urban greenery can be a part of a strategy to lure investment and drive economic growth that concurrently increases property values and quality of life in the city. Real estate premiums are common among residential buildings in close proximity to either large, formal parks or small, vegetated pocket parks.[8][9] This points out the need for careful attention to relative impact of increased hedonic value of real estate while ensuring equitable access for the broader community.

Housing developments with large trees have been found to attract people to be outdoors, talk with neighbours and develop stronger social bonds.[10] Neighbourhood greenery and access to parks has also been correlated to fewer felonies,[11] reduced aggression and violence, mental fatigue, outbursts of anger and prevalence of some types of domestic violence as well as increased attention span and reliability. [12]

FIGURE 12.2 SANTIAGO CALATRAVA, BROOKFIELD PLACE, TORONTO, CANADA, 1992. The Allen Lambert Galleria stitches together several building façades to create a pedestrian thoroughfare. The soaring, light-filled atrium induces a sense of awe and supports a strong prospect view through the space, further accentuated with a dynamic lighting scheme.

CASE STUDY 12.1:
RECLAIMING URBAN SPACES

FIGURE 12.3 DILLER SCOFIDIO + RENFRO WITH JAMES CORNER FIELD OPERATIONS AND PIET OUDOLF, THE HIGH LINE, NEW YORK CITY, 2009–19, AND ADJACENT OFFICE BUILDING BY COOKFOX ARCHITECTS, 512 WEST 22ND STREET, 2019. The variety of spatial and planting experiences, has prompted new development all along this urban corridor. 512 West 22nd Street was designed specifically to visually connect with the High Line, from planted terraces that cut into the façade, to exterior stairways and interior office space looking north and south along the park.

Near the Hudson River on the west side of Manhattan in New York City is the High Line, one of the most well known examples re-envisioning urban infrastructure. The decommissioned elevated railway came close to being demolished before a small group of advocates championed the concept of a public park. Inspired by the conversion of a rail viaduct in Paris into Coulée verte René–Dumont linear park, the High Line project turned a 2.33km (1.45 mile) long former elevated railroad spur into a vibrant public park with forest groves, seating areas and performance spaces.

The park was projected to attract 300,000 annual visitors when it opened in 2009, yet it received 1.3 million visitors, and by 2015 that number had increased to 7.6 million.[13] The High Line's elevated linear park has become one of the most visited landmarks in New York. The former warehouse and art gallery district has experienced a jump in retail sales, hotel rates and redevelopment. Residential property values within half a kilometre of the park jumped 10% in the first year and, by 2010, the increase in property taxes was estimated to be more than the cost of construction of the park.[14]

CASE STUDY 12.2:
EVOKING REMEMBRANCES OF PLACE

Central Sydney, Australia, has become vertiginous and the narrow sidewalks overcrowded. The city decided to clean up and enliven service laneways to create more pedestrian routes through the precinct. Overhead in one alley are a number of antique-looking metal birdcages, while below paving stones are engraved with bird names. While walking through the alley the occasional songbird can be heard, even though the cages are empty. This is the sound of *Forgotten Songs,* a public art installation that commemorates the songs of 50 birds once prevalent in what is now central Sydney, before they were gradually forced out by European settlement. The birdsongs are only played at the time of day and time of year in which those species would have sang those songs. The installation has proved immensely popular, transforming the alley it occupies.

Forgotten Songs may be one of the first biophilic design projects that is both site-specific and replicable — a feat which has proven to be one of the greatest challenges among designers, planners and others looking to address issues of urbanisation, climate change and habitat loss, while also reconnecting urban dwellers with nature and possibly improve their perception of well-being and environmental stewardship.

FIGURE 12.4 MICHAEL THOMAS HILL, FORGOTTEN SONGS, ANGEL PLACE, SYDNEY, AUSTRALIA, 2011. The songs of extinct and extirpated birds that were prevalent in what is now central Sydney, haunt the mid–block laneway. This compelling work was originally intended to be a temporary art installation, but due to its popularity was remade as a permanent part of Angel Place.

CASE STUDY 12.3:
INTENSIFIED RESTORATION

Designed by Robert Zion, Paley Park in New York City — the first pocket park of its kind — opened in May 1967. It is tiny, 390m2 (4,200ft2), this tiny park opens onto the street to the north with the east and west walls covered with ivy. The north wall is dominated by a 6.1m (20ft) tall waterfall — the focal point for the space. Honey locust trees are planted between rough-hewn stone tiles, creating an amazing dappled light in the park. Moveable marble-topped tables and lattice-wired chairs throughout the space allow for flexible configurations and proximity to the misting waterfall. It is, in effect, an outdoor room.

Located in the commercial heart of New York City this public space, on privately owned land, receives over 500,000 visitors per year. Very few of the tall buildings nearby provide usable outdoor areas, and Central Park is too far to reach for a short break. Paley Park is a unique oasis for nearby office workers and museum patrons. A small coffee shop sits tucked away in the southeast corner.

Approximately 20% of the total floor and wall area is occupied by the park's waterfall, and its sound can be heard from the sidewalk of 53rd Street, well before seeing the entrance to the park. At up to 90 decibels, it is loud enough to drown out traffic and other street noises, as well as neighbouring conversations.

Informal surveys of park visitors revealed a commonality of sentiments or phrases used to describe Paley Park, such as having an 'oasis in the city' feel and a 'quiet atmosphere', as well as offering a collective change in mood, increased happiness and perceived reduction in stress.[15] These self-reported qualitative changes, along with consistent usage patterns, show a strong indication of the success of the park.

FIGURE 12.5 ZION BREEN RICHARDSON
ASSOCIATES, PALEY PARK, EAST 53RD STREET,
NEW YORK CITY, USA, 1967. Paley Park creates a
strong visual connection to nature, has beautiful
dynamic light and is dominated by a central
waterfall. This first of a kind 'pocket park' is
occupied almost any time the gates are open, with
the exception of the few times when the waterfall
is turned off.

FIGURE 12.6 PATRICK JACOBS, DANDELION CLUSTER #3, MUSEUM OF ARTS AND DESIGN, COLUMBUS CIRCLE, NEW YORK CITY, USA, 2011. On a wall adjoining busy Columbus Circle (a–b) is a portal to a miniature landscape. (c) A type of urban biophilic acupuncture, the nanoscape diorama viewed through a two–inch window lures passers–by with a sense of mystery, curiosity, joy and awe, to revel in a micro–restorative break from the hectic streetscape.

CLOSING THOUGHTS

There are a number of lessons to reflect on from the examples in this book. The evolution of space design in the COOKFOX architectural offices reflects the value of post-occupancy work to inform biophilic design. The presence of biophilic design can change the usage patterns of spaces, as evidenced by the increased number of active and passive users in hotel lobbies at citizenM; or it can enable the repositioning of a brand, as seen with the PARKROYAL on Pickering. Biophilic design is applicable to historically designated buildings, whether through preservation such as at the Hilton Netherland Plaza Hotel in Cincinnati, or through renovation such as with the Interface showroom in Krefeld.

Biophilic design is incredibly effective for themed or immersive spaces like the Le Comptoir TRi restaurant in Hong Kong, Restoration Hardware in Atlanta and Seesaw Coffee in Beijing. The Garden School Hackney and the Baltimore Green Street Academy examples demonstrate that even minimal interior interventions can improve outcomes. The Sasanqua Spa and Johnson Wax examples show that thoughtful biophilic design can produce a space that ages gracefully and is beloved to the point where it stays intact for decades, a true measure of sustainability.

Biophilic design brings a new level of intention to design — a lens through which the scope of design expands beyond function and beauty. Knowing that biophilic design can measurably support positive psychological and physiological conditions presents a new frontier of responsibility and purpose to the profession.

Biophilic design is one of many components of a holistic approach to buildings and places. It can be a powerful tool to support human health and well-being in the built environment. There are many other things that support our health and well-being, and they need to be addressed as well. Hopefully biophilic experiences in buildings will also engender an awareness and desire to nurture natural environments.

While bringing nature inside can help to create meaningful and enduring experiences of the built environment, ultimately the most important suggestion we can make is to get outdoors and directly engage with nature.

FIGURE A.0 ETCHED PORCELAIN LAMPSHADE

FUNDAMENTAL PARAMETERS
FOR VISUAL PERCEPTION

Visual perception relies on the capacity of the human eye to focus in response to its environment. Vision in the near focal length requires the muscles of the eye to contract the lens. With a distant view, the lens flattens and the muscles relax. Periodic access to greater view depths (Figure A.1a) helps to reduce eye strain and related discomforts, while also supporting decision–making and connection to place (e.g. time of day, weather, workplace activity).

The peripheral zones in the field of vision (Figure A.1b) are the best areas to place non–rhythmic sensory stimuli, such as water features, or tall grasses that move with natural or mechanical ventilation. Movement in the peripheral zone is perceived much faster than movement from directly ahead. The far periphery (≥170° and ≤10°) is also an acceptable default range for creating a basic refuge condition.

DEPTH OF VISION

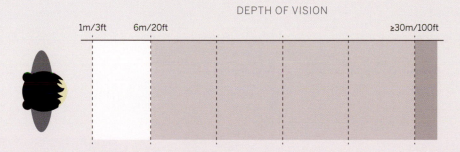

FIGURE A.1A Focal lengths.

FIELD OF VISION

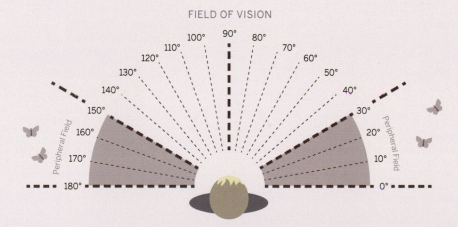

FIGURE A.1B Peripheral field of vision.

FUNDAMENTAL PARAMETERS
FOR DESIGNING WITH FRACTALS

Fractals are geometric objects or shapes that exhibit self-similarity across scales. Familiar natural phenomena with fractal features include trees, snowflakes and frost crystals, ferns, pineapples, river networks, clouds and lightning. Over time, humans have adapted to more easily, efficiently and fluidly process naturally-occurring fractal patterns. This adaptation is known as the **fractal fluency theory**. With this adaptation, observing fractals characteristic of those most commonly occurring in nature can lead to a measurable decrease in stress levels.

Exact fractals have a self-repeating pattern. The number of repeats or the scaling factor makes a difference in our biological response and interest. A basic square fractal gasket (Figure A.2a) becomes more complex as the number of repeats or iterations increases. Balance in the creation of fractals is important because more than three repetitions can sometimes create aggressive forms that may induce a stress or fear response among some people.

Statistical fractals show the same statistical properties at different scales. Fractal dimension (an integer quantity or fractional value, whereby D = 1.0–1.9) is a measurement of how quickly length, area or volume change with decreasing scale. Different fractal dimensions are known to influence our perception and engage interest to varying degrees. Fractals of low value (D < 1.3) are of less interest to the eye high values (D > 1.7) tend to engender stress in some people and creativity in others. Mid-range fractals (D = 1.3–1.7) are considered the most engaging and interesting in nature. The software and scripts needed to calculate dimensions of existing spaces or products are not yet readily available for direct design application, but looking to familiar examples in nature can be a good place to start (Figure A.2b).

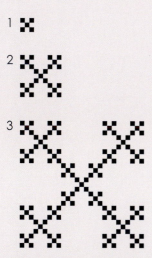

FIGURE A.2A Example of an exact or regular fractal gasket.

FIGURE A.2B A series of distinctly different statistical fractals created by the same variables — daylight, passing through trees, hitting the ground.

B. DECISION TIMELINE FOR BIOPHILIC DESIGN INTEGRATION

The point at which biophilic design concepts are introduced on a project could significantly influence feasibility and efficacy. Yet with so many opportunities for incorporating nature and health goals, every project schedule may reflect different priorities. This schedule offers high-level objectives and actions that could be adapted for any project.

FUNDAMENTAL STRATEGIES integral to the overall biophilic experience and perception of a space or place		OPTIMIZATION OF STRATEGIES to align with indoor environmental quality and other priorities		MINOR INTERVENTIONS to supplement the biophilic experience	

OBJECTIVE

| **Assess** existing biophilic conditions of the site or building. What landscape or climatic conditions or adjacencies can be easily or freely leveraged for the benefit of the project and future occupants. | | **Engage** other disciplines and subject matter experts in biophilic design strategy; identify how each discipline could contribute to achieving the desired biophilic experience. | | **Track** specifications and purchasing; confirm possible substitutes are able to retain intended biophilic experience. | **Observe** space utilisation and maintain intended biophilic experiences over time. |

SITE SELECTION & DUE DILIGENCE	CONCEPT DESIGN	SCHEMATIC DESIGN	DESIGN DEVELOPMENT	CONSTRUCTION DOCS TO CLOSE OUT	OCCUPANCY & OPERATIONS

ACTION

| Identify primary desired outcomes and biophilic patterns and experiences to be integrated into the overall Project Concept and **Owner Project Requirements**. | | Conduct **biophilic design peer reviews** to ensure design continuously upholds experiential goals. | | Include biophilic design items on **punch list** to confirm efficacy of installation. | **Share design intent** with facility managers and occupants. |

C. HEALTH OUTCOMES CHART

BIOPHILIC DESIGN PATTERN	IMPROVED PHYSIOLOGICAL RESPONSE	IMPROVED COGNITIVE FUNCTIONING	EMOTIONS AND MOOD AND PREFERENCE
VISUAL CONNECTION WITH NATURE	– **Lowered blood pressure and heart rate** (Hartig et al., 2003; Lee et al., 2009; Li & Sullivan, 2016; Song et al., 2016; Tsunetsugu & Miyazaki, 2005; van den Berg, Hartig, & Staats, 2007; Yin et al., 2018) – **Increased parasympathetic activity** (Brown, Barton & Gladwell, 2013)	– **Improved mental engagement/ attentiveness** (Lee et al., 2015; Biederman & Vessel, 2006; Li & Sullivan, 2016; Mayer et al., 2009)	– **Positively impacted attitude and overall happiness** (Barton & Pretty, 2010; Hartig et al., 2003; An et al., 2016; Mayer et al., 2009) – **Reduced future discounting** (van der Wal et al., 2013) – **Heightened appreciation for nature** (Mayer et al., 2009) – **Decreased rumination** (Bratman et al., 2015) – **Correlation between view preference and motivation** (Yue, Vessel & Biederman, 2007)
NON–VISUAL CONNECTION TO NATURE	– **Reduced systolic blood pressure and stress hormones** (Annerstedt et al., 2013; Alvarsson et al., 2010; Li et al., 2012) – **Improved immune function** (Li et al., 2012)	– **Positively impacted cognitive performance** (Haapakangas et al., 2011; Abbott et al., 2016; Van Hedger et al., 2019; Warm, Dember, & Parasuraman, 1991) – **Improved creativity** (Haapakangas et al., 2011)	– **Perceived improvements in mental health, tranquillity and pain management** (Alvarsson et al., 2010; Benfield et al., 2014; Pheasant et al., 2010; Watts et al., 2009; Krzywicka & Byrka, 2017; Jahncke, et al., 2011; Tsunetsugu, Park & Miyazaki, 2010; Kim et al., 2007) – **Observed preference** (Haapakangas et al., 2011)
NON–RHYTHMIC SENSORY STIMULI	– **Positively impacted heart rate, systolic blood pressure and sympathetic nervous system activity** (Beauchamp et al., 2003; Ulrich, Simons, Losito et al., 1991)		– **Increased dwell time and observed behavioral measures of attention and exploration** (Windhager et al., 2011)
THERMAL AND AIRFLOW VARIABILITY	– **Positively impacted comfort, well–being and productivity** (Heerwagen, 2006; Wigö, 2005) – **Fewer self–reported Sick Building Syndrome cases** (Tham & Willem, 2005)	– **Improved task performance** (Tham & Willem, 2005; Wigö, 2005)	– **Improved perception of temporal and spatial pleasure (alliesthesia)** (Parkinson, de Dear & Candido, 2012; Zhang, Arens, Huizenga & Han, 2010; Arens, Zhang & Huizenga, 2006; Zhang, 2003; de Dear & Brager, 2002; Heschong, 1979)
PRESENCE OF WATER	– **Reduced stress, increased feelings of tranquillity, lowered heart rate and blood pressure** (Galbrun & Ali, 2013; Alvarsson, Wiens, & Nilsson, 2010; Annerstedt et al., 2013; Haapakangas et al., 2011; Pheasant et al., 2010)	– **Positively impacted cognitive performance and creativity** (Haapakangas et al., 2011)	– **Observed preferences and positive emotional responses** (Haapakangas et al., 2011; Jahncke et al., 2011; Hunter et al., 2010; Windhager, 2011; Barton & Pretty, 2010; White, Smith, Humphryes et al., 2010; Karmanov & Hamel, 2008; Ruso & Atzwanger, 2003; Watts et al., 2009; Biederman & Vessel, 2006)
DYNAMIC AND DIFFUSE LIGHT	– **Positively impacted circadian system functioning** (Elzeyadi, 2011; Figueiro, Brons, Plitnick et al., 2011; Figueiro et al., 2017; Figueiro et al., 2018; Boubekri et al., 2014) – **Increased visual comfort** (Elzeyadi, 2012)	– **Improved cognitive and behavioral performance** (Keis et al., 2014; Mott et al., 2012; Mott et al., 2014; Boubekri et al., 2014)	– **Positively impacted attitude and overall happiness** (An et al., 2016)

BIOPHILIC DESIGN PATTERN	IMPROVED PHYSIOLOGICAL RESPONSE	IMPROVED COGNITIVE FUNCTIONING	EMOTIONS AND MOOD AND PREFERENCE
CONNECTION WITH NATURAL SYSTEMS	– **Enhanced positive health responses** – **Shifted perception of environment** (Kellert et al., 2008)		– **Enhanced positive health responses; Shifted perception of environment** (Kellert et al., 2008)
BIOMORPHIC FORMS AND PATTERNS	– **Improved stress recovery** (Determan et al., 2019)	– **Improved learning outcomes** (Determan et al., 2019)	– **Observed view preference** (Joye, 2007; Kardan et al., 2015)
MATERIAL CONNECTION WITH NATURE	– **Decreased diastolic blood pressure; Improved comfort** (Tsunetsugu, Miyazaki & Sato, 2007) – **Reduced plasma cortisol level** (Ohta et al., 2008) – **Increased heart rate variability** (Kelz, Grote & Moser, 2011) – **Self–reported calming effect** (Rice et al., 2006)	– **Improved cognitive performance and self–reported productivity** (Shen, Zhang & Lian, 2020)	– **Observed material preference** (Jimenez et al., 2016; Nyrud & Bringslimark, 2010; Berger, Katz & Petutschnigg, 2006; Rice et al., 2006)
COMPLEXITY & ORDER	– **Positively impacted perceptual and physiological stress responses** (Hägerhäll et al. 2015, Salingaros, 2012; Joye, 2007; Taylor, 2006; Determan et al., 2019)	– **Brainwave response indicative of relaxation** (Hägerhäll et al., 2008) – **Improved environmental navigation** (Juliani et al., 2016) – **Improved learning outcomes** (Determan et al., 2019)	– **Subjective positive mood and preference response** (Abboushi et al., 2019; Bies et al., 2016; Salingaros, 2012; Hägerhäll, Laike, Taylor et al., 2008; Hägerhäll, Purcella, & Taylor, 2004; Taylor, 2006)
PROSPECT	– **Reduced stress** (Grahn & Stigsdotter, 2010) – **Improved comfort and perceived safety** (Herzog & Bryce, 2007; Wang & Taylor, 2006; Petherick, 2000)		– **Reduced boredom, irritation, fatigue** (Clearwater & Coss, 1991) – **Visual preference** (Wiener et al., 2007; Mumcu, Duzenli & Özbilen, 2010)
REFUGE	– **Improved perception of safety** (Petherick, 2000)		– **Observed visual preference** (Grahn & Stigsdotter, 2010; Petherick, 2000)
MYSTERY			– **Observed visual preference** (Herzog & Bryce, 2007; Kent, 1989) – **Induced strong pleasure response** (Ikemi, 2005)
RISK / PERIL			– **Heightened dopamine or pleasure responses** (Kohno et al., 2015; Wang & Tsien, 2011)
AWE	– **Reduced stress–related symptoms** (Anderson, Monroy & Keltner, 2018)		– **Increased pro–social behaviour** (Anderson, Monroy & Keltner, 2018; Piff et al., 2015; Stellar et al., 2015; S tellar et al., 2018) – **Positively impacted attitude and overall happiness** (Anderson, Monroy 2018)

HEALTH OUTCOMES CHART – BIBLIOGRAPHY

Abbott, L.C., Taff, D., Newman, P., Benfield, J.A., Mowen, A.J.; 'The influence of natural sounds on attention restoration', *The Journal of Park and Recreation Administration*, Vol. 34, issue 3, 2016. https://doi.org/10.18666/JPRA-2016-V34-I3-6893

Abboushi, B., Elzeyadi, I., Taylor, R., Sereno, M.; 'Fractals in architecture: The visual interest, preference & mood response to projected fractal light patterns in interior spaces', *Journal of Environmental Psychology*, 61, 2019, pp. 57-70.

Alvarsson, J., Wiens, S., Nilsson, N.; 'Stress Recovery during Exposure to Nature Sound and Environmental Noise', *International Journal of Environmental Research and Public Health*, Vol. 7, issue 3, 2010, pp. 1036-1046.

An, M., Colarelli, S.M., O'Brien, K., Boyajian, M.E.; 'Why we need more nature at work: Effects of natural elements and sunlight on employee mental health and work attitudes', *PLoS ONE*, Vol. 11, issue 5, 2016. DOI: 10.1371/journal.pone.0155614

Annerstedt, M., Jonsson, P., Wallergard, M., Johansson, G., Karlson, B., Grahn, Patrik, Hansen, Ase, M., Wahrborg, P.; 'Inducing physiological stress recovery with sounds of nature in a virtual reality forest: Results from a pilot study', *Physiology & Behavior*, Vol. 118, 2013, pp. 240-250.

Anderson, C.L., Monroy, M., Keltner, D.; 'Awe in nature heals: Evidence from military veterans, at-risk youth, and college students', *Emotion*, Vol. 18, issue 8, 2018, pp. 1195-1202. http://dx.doi.org/10.1037/emo0000442

Arens, E., Zhang H., Huizenga, C.; 'Partial- and Whole-body Thermal Sensation and Comfort, Part II: Non-uniform Environmental Conditions,' *Journal of Thermal Biology*, Vol. 31, 2006, pp. 60-66.

Barton, J., Pretty J.; 'What Is the Best Dose of Nature and Green Exercise for Improving Mental Health', *Environmental Science & Technology*, Vol. 44, 2010, pp. 3947–3955.

Beauchamp, M.S., Lee K.E., Haxby, J.V., Martin, J.V.; 'FMRI Responses to Video and Point-Light Displays of Moving Humans and Manipulable Objects', *Journal of Cognitive Neuroscience*, Vol. 15, issue 7, 2003, pp. 991–1001.

Benfield, J.A., Taff, D.B., Newman, P., Smyth, J.; 'Natural sound facilitates mood recovery', *Ecopsychology*, Vol. 6 issue 3, 2014. DOI: 10.1089/eco.2014.0028

Berger, G., Katz, H., Petutschnigg, A.J.; 'What consumers feel and prefer: haptic perception of various wood flooring surfaces', *Forest Products Journal*, Vol. 56, issue. 10, 2006.

Biederman, I., Vessel, E.; 'Perceptual Pleasure & the Brain', *American Scientist*, Vol. 94, issue 1, 2006, pp. 249-255.

Bies, A.J., Blanc-Goldhammer, D.R., Boydston, C.R., Taylor, R.P., Sereno, M.E.; 'Aesthetic response to exact fractals driven by physical complexity', *Frontiers in Human Neuroscience*, Vol. 10, 2016. DOI:10.3389/fnhum.2016.00210

Boubekri, M., Chueng, I.N., Reid, K.J., Wang, C., Zee, P.H.; 'Impact of Windows and Daylight Exposure on Overall Health and Sleep Quality of Office Workers: A Case-Control Pilot Study', *Journal of Clinical Sleep Medicine*, Vol. 10, issue 6, 2014, pp. 603-11.

Bratman, G.N., Hamilton, J.P., Hahn, K.S., Daily, G.C., Gross, J.J.; 'Nature experience reduces rumination and subgenual prefrontal cortex activation', *Proceedings of the National Academy of Sciences*, Vol. 112, issue 28, 2015, pp. 8567–8572. https://doi.org/10.1073/pnas.1510459112

Brown, D.K., Barton, J.L., Gladwell, V.F.; 'Viewing Nature Scenes Positively Affects Recovery of Autonomic Function Following Acute-Mental Stress', *Environmental Science & Technology*, Vol. 47, 2013, pp. 5562-5569.

Clearwater, Y.A., Coss, R.G.; 'Functional esthetics to enhance wellbeing' in *From Antarctica to Outer Space: Life in Isolation and Confinement*, eds. A. Harrison, Y. Clearwater & C. McKay, Springer-Verlag, New York, 1991, pp. 331-348.

de Dear, R., Brager, G.; Thermal comfort in naturally ventilated buildings, *Energy and Buildings*, Vol. 34, 2002, 549-561.

Determan, J., Albright, T., Browning, W., Akers, M.A., Archibald, P., Martin-Dunlop, C., Caruolo, V.; 'The Impact of Biophilic Design on Student Success', *AIA BRIK*, November 2019.

Elzeyadi, I.; 'Daylighting-Bias and Biophilia: Quantifying the Impacts of Daylight on Occupants Health', in Greenbuild 2011 Proceedings, Thought and Leadership in Green Buildings Research, USGBC Press, Washington, DC, 2011.

Elzeyadi, I.M.K.; 'Quantifying the Impacts of Green Schools on People and Planet', in Proceedings of the 2012 Greenbuild Conference, San Francisco, 2012, pp.48-60.

Figueiro, M.G., Steverson, B., Heerwagen, J., Kampschroer, K., Hunter, C.M., Gonzales, K., Plitnick, B., Rea, M.S.; 'The impact of daytime light exposures on sleep and mood in office workers', *Sleep Health: Journal of the National Sleep Foundation*, Vol. 3, issue 3, 2017, pp. 204-215.

Figueiro, M.G., Kalsher, M., Steverson, B., Heerwagen, J., Kampschroer, K., Rea, M.S.; 'Circadian-effective light and its impact on alertness in office workers', *Lighting Research and Technology*, Vol. 0, 2018, pp. 1-13.

Figueiro, M.G., Brons, J.A., Plitnick, B., Donlan, B., Leslie, R.P., Rea M.S.; 'Measuring circadian light and its impact on adolescents', *Lighting Research & Technology*, Vol 43, issue 2, 2011, pp. 201-215.

Galbrun, L., Ali, T.T.; 'Acoustical and perceptual assessment of water sounds and their use over road traffic noise', *Journal of the Acoustical Society of America*, Vol. 133, issue 1, 2013, pp. 227-237. DOI: 10.1121/1.4770242

Grahn, P., Stigsdotter, U.K.; 'The Relation Between Perceived Sensory Dimensions of Urban Green Space and Stress Restoration', *Landscape and Urban Planning*, Vol. 94, 2010, pp. 264-275.

Haapakangas, A., Kankkunen, E., Hongisto, V., Virjonen, P., Keskinen, E.; 'Effects of Five Speech Masking Sounds on Performance and Acoustic Satisfaction. Implications for Open-Plan Offices', *ACTA Acustica United with Acustica*, Vol. 97, 2011, pp. 641-655.

Hägerhäll, C.M., Laike,T., Taylor R., Küller, M., Küller, R., Martin, T.P.; 'Investigations of Human EEG Response to Viewing Fractal Patterns', *Perception*, Vol. 37, 2008, pp. 1488-1494.

Hägerhäll, C., Laike, T., Kuller, M., Marcheschi, E., Boydston, C., Taylor, R.; Human Physiological Benefits of Viewing Nature: EEG Responses to Exact and Statistical Fractal Patterns, *Nonlinear dynamics, psychology, and life sciences*, Vol. 19, 2015, pp. 1-12.

Hägerhäll, C.M., Purcella, T., Taylor, R.; 'Fractal Dimension of Landscape Silhouette Outlines as a Predictor of Landscape Preference', *Journal of Environmental Psychology*, Vol. 24, 2004, pp. 247-255.

Hartig, T., Evans, G.W., Jamner, L.D., Davis, D.S., Gärling, T.; 'Tracking Restoration in Natural and Urban Field Settings', *Journal of Environmental Psychology*, Vol. 23, 2003, pp. 109–123.

Heerwagen, J.H.; 'Investing In People: The Social Benefits of Sustainable Design. Rethinking Sustainable Construction' Sarasota, FL. September 19- 22, 2006.

Heschong, L.; *Thermal Delight in Architecture*, MIT Press, Cambridge, MA, 1979.

Herzog, T.R., Bryce, A.G.; 'Mystery and Preference in Within-Forest Settings', *Environment and Behavior*, Vol. 39, issue 6, 2007, pp. 779-796.

Hunter, M.D., Eickhoff, S.B., Pheasant, R.J., Douglas, M.J., Watts, G.R., Farrow, T.F.D., Hyland, D., Kang, J., Wilkinson, I.D., Horoshenkov, K.V., Woodruff, P.W.R; 'The state of tranquility: Subjective perception is shaped by contextual modulation of auditory connectivity', *Neuroimage*, Vol. 53, 2010, pp. 611–618.

Ikemi M.; 'The effects of mystery on preference for residential façades', *Journal of Environmental Psychology*, Vol. 25, 2005, pp. 167–173.

Jahncke, H., Hygge, S., Lahin, N., Green, A.M., Dimberg, K.; 'Open-plan office noise: Cognitive performance and restoration', *Journal of Environmental Psychology*, Vol. 31, 2011, pp. 501–509.

Jiménez, P., Dunkl, A., Eibel, K., Denk, E., Grote, V., Kelz C., Moser, M.; 'Wood or Laminate?—Psychological Research of Customer Expectations', *Forests*, Vol. 7, issue 11, 2016. DOI: 10.3390/f7110275

Joye, Y.; 'Architectural Lessons from Environmental Psychology: The Case of Biophilic Architecture', *Review of General Psychology*, Vol. 11, issue 4, 2007, pp. 305-328.

Juliani, A.W., Bies, A.J., Boydston, C.R., Taylor, R.P., Sereno, M.E.; 'Navigation performance in virtual environments varies with fractal dimension of landscape', *Journal of Environmental Psychology*, Vol. 47, 2016, pp. 155-165.

Kardan, O., Demiralp, E., Hout, M.C., Hunter, M.R., Karimi, H., Hanayik, T., Yourganov, G., Jonides, J., Berman, M.G.; 'Is the preference for natural versus man-made scenes driven by bottom-up processing of the visual features of nature?', *Frontiers in Psychology*, Vol. 6, article 471, 2015. DOI: 10.3389/fpsyg.2015.00471

Karmanov, D., Hamel, R.; 'Assessing the restorative potential of contemporary urban environment(s)', *Landscape and Urban Planning*, Vol. 86, 2008, pp. 115-125.

Keis, O., Helbig, H., Streb, J., Hille, K.; 'Influence of blue-enriched classroom lighting on students' cognitive performance', *Trends in Neuroscience and Education*, Vol. 3, issue 3, 2014, pp. 86-92. http://dx.doi.org/10.1016/j.tine.2014.09.001

Kellert, S.R., Heerwagen, J.H., Mador, M.L. Eds.; *Biophilic Design: The Theory, Science & Practice of Bringing Buildings to Life*, John Wiley & Sons, Hoboken, NJ, 2008.

Kelz, C., Grote, V., & Moser, M.; 'Interior Wood Use in Classrooms Reduces Pupils' Stress Levels', *Proceedings of the 9th Biennial Conference on Environmental Psychology,* Eindhoven Technical University, 2011.

Kent, R.L.; 'The Role of Mystery in Preferences for Shopping Malls', *Landscape Journal*, Vol. 8, 1989, pp. 28-35.

Kim, J.T., Ren, C.J., Fielding, G.A., Pitti, A., Kasumi, T., Wajda, M., Lebovits, A., Bekker, A.; 'Treatment with Lavender Aromatherapy in the Post Anesthesia Care Unit Reduces Opioid Requirements of Morbidly Obese Patients Undergoing Laparoscopic Adjustable Gastric Banding', *Obesity Surgery*, Vol. 17, issue 7, 2007, pp. 920-925.

Kohno, M., Ghahremani, D.G., Morales, A.M., Robertson, C.L., Ishibashi, K., Morgan, A.T., Mandelkern, M.A., London, E.D.; 'Risk-taking behavior: Dopamine D2/D3 receptors, feedback, and frontolimbic activity', *Cerebral Cortex*, Vol. 25, 2015, pp. 236-245.

Kryzwicka, P., Byrka, K.; 'Restorative qualities of and preference for natural and urban soundscapes', *Frontiers in Psychology*, Vol. 8, 2017. DOI: 10.3389/fpsyg.2017.01705

Lee, J., Park, B.J., Tsunetsugu, Y., Kagawa, T., Miyazaki, Y.; 'Restorative effects of viewing real forest landscapes, based on a comparison with urban landscapes', *Scandinavian Journal of Forest Research*, Vol. 24: 2009, pp. 227–234. DOI: 10.1080/02827580902903341

Lee, K.E., Williams, K.J.H., Sargent, L.D., Williams, N.S.G., Johnson, K.A.; '40-second green roof views sustain attention: The role of micro-breaks in attention restoration', *Journal of Environmental Psychology*, Vol. 42, 2015, pp. 182-189.

Li, D., Sullivan, W.C.; 'Impact of views to school landscapes on recovery from stress and mental fatigue', *Landscape and Urban Planning*, Vol. 148, 2016, pp. 149-158.

Li, Q., Kobayashi, M., Inagaki, H., Wakayama, Y., Katsumata, M., Hirata, Y., Li, Y., Hirata, K., Shimizu, T., Nakadai, A., Kawada, T.; 'Effect of Phytoncides from Forest Environments on Immune Function' in Forest Medicine, ed. Q. Li Nova Science Publishers, Hauppauge, NY, 2012, pp. 157-167.

Mayer, F.S., Frantz, C., Bruehlman-Senecal E., Dolliver, K.; 'Why Is Nature Beneficial? The Role of Connectedness to Nature', *Environment and Behavior*, Vol. 41, issue 5, 2009, pp. 607-643. DOI: 10.1177/0013916508319745

Mott, M.S., Robinson, D.H., Walden, A., Burnette, J., Rutherford, A.S.; 'Illuminating the effects of dynamic lighting on student learning', *Sage Open*, Vol. 2, issue 2, 2012. DOI: 10.1177/2158244012445585

Mott, M.S., Robinson, D.H., Williams-Black, T.H., McClelland, S.S.; 'The supporting effects of high luminous conditions on grade 3 oral reading fluency scores', *SpringerPlus*, Vol. 3, Article 53, 2014. DOI: 10.1186/2193-1801-3-53

Mumcu, S., Duzenli, T., Özbilen, A.; 'Prospect and refuge as the predictors of preferences for seating areas', *Scientific Research and Essays*, Vol. 5, 2011, pp. 1223-1233.

Nyrud, A.Q., Bringslimark, T.; 'Is interior wood use psychologically beneficial? A review of psychological responses toward wood', *Wood and Fiber Science*, Vol. 42, issue 2, 2010, pp. 202-218.

Ohta, H., Marutama, M., Tanabe, Y., Hara, T., Nishino, Y., Tsujino, Y., Morita, E., Kobayashi, S., Shido, O.; 'Effects of Redecoration of a Hospital Isolation Room with Natural Materials on Stress Levels of Denizens in Cold Season', *International Journal of Biometeorology*, Vol. 52, 2008, pp. 331-340.

Parkinson, T., de Dear, R., Candido, C.; 'Perception of Transient Thermal Environments: Pleasure and Alliesthesia', *Proceedings of 7th Windsor Conference*, Windsor, UK, 2012.

Petherick, N.; 'Environmental design and fear: The prospect-refuge model and the university college of the cariboo campus', *Western Geography*, Vol. 10, issue 1, 2000, pp. 89-112.

Pheasant, R.J., Fisher, M.N., Watts, G.R., Whitaker, D.J., Horoshenkov, K.V.; 'The importance of auditory-visual interaction in the construction of 'tranquil space', *Journal of Environmental Psychology*, Vol. 30, 2010, pp. 501–509.

Piff, P.K., Dietze, P., Feinberg, M., DStancato, D.M., Keltner, D.; 'Awe, the small self, and prosocial behavior', *Journal of Personality and Social Psychology*, Vol. 108, issue 6, 2015, pp. 883-899. http://dx.doi.org/10.1037/pspi0000018

Rice, J., Kozak, R.A., Meitner, M.J., Cohen, D.H.; 'Appearance of wood products and psychological well-being', *Wood and Fiber Science*, Vol. 38, issue 4, 2006, pp. 644-659.

Ruso, B., Atzwanger, K.; 'Measuring Immediate Behavioural Responses to the Environment', *The Michigan Psychologist*, Vol. 4, 2003, p. 12.

Salingaros, N.A.; 'Fractal Art and Architecture Reduce Physiological Stress', *Journal of Biourbanism*, Vol. 2, issue 2, 2012, pp. 11-28.

Shen, J.Y., Zhang X., Lian, Z.W.; 'Impact of wooden versus nonwooden interior designs on office workers' cognitive performance', *Perceptual and Motor Skills*, Vol. 127, issue 1, 2020, pp. 36–51.

Stellar, J.E., Gordon, A., Anderson, C.L., Piff, P.K., McNeil, G.D., Keltner, D.; Awe and humility', *Journal of Personality and Social Psychology*, Vol. 114, issue 2, 2018, pp. 258-269. http://dx.doi.org/10.1037/pspi0000109

Stellar, J.E., John-Henderson, N., Anderson, C.L., Gordon, A.M., McNeil, G.D., Keltner, D.; 'Positive affect and markers of inflammation: Discrete positive emotions predict lower levels of inflammatory cytokines', *Emotion*, Vol. 15, issue 2, 2015, pp. 129-133. http://dx.doi.org/10.1037/emo0000033

Song, C., Ikei, H., Kobayashi, M., Miura, T., Li, Q., Kagawa, T., Kumeda, S., Imaif, M., Miyazaki, Y.; 'Effects of viewing forest landscape on middle-aged hypertensive men', *Urban Forestry & Urban Greening*, Vol. 21, 2016, pp. 247-252.

Tallis, H., Bratman, G.N., Samhouri, J.F., Fargione, J.; 'Are California elementary school test scores more strongly associated with urban trees than poverty?', *Frontiers in Psychology*, Vol. 9, 2018. https://doi.org/10.3389/fpsyg.2018.02074.

Taylor, R.P., 'Reduction of Physiological Stress Using Fractal Art and Architecture', *Leonardo*, Vol. 39, issue 3, 2006, pp. 245–251.

Tham, K.W., Willem, H.C.; 'Temperature and Ventilation Effects on Performance and Neurobehavioral-Related Symptoms of Tropically Acclimatized Call Center Operators Near Thermal Neutrality', *ASHRAE Transactions*, 2005, pp. 687-698.

Tsunetsugu, Y., Miyazaki, Y.; 'Measurement of Absolute Hemoglobin Concentrations of Prefrontal Region by Near-Infrared Time-Resolved Spectroscopy: Examples of Experiments and Prospects', *Journal of Physiological Anthropology and Applied Human Science*, Vol. 24, issue 4, 2005, pp. 469-72.

Tsunetsugu, Y., Park, B.J., Miyazaki Y.; 'Trends in research related to "Shinrin-yoku" (taking in the forest atmosphere or forest bathing)', *Environmental Health & Preventive Medicine*, Vol. 15, 2010, pp. 27–37.

Tsunetsugu, Y., Miyazaki, Y., Sato, H.; 'Physiological Effects in Humans Induced by the Visual Stimulation of Room Interiors with Different Wood Quantities', *Journal of Wood Science*, Vol. 53, issue 1, 2007, pp. 11-16.

Ulrich, R.S., Simons, R.F., Losito, B.D., Fiorito, E., Miles, M.A., Zelson, M.; 'Stress recovery during exposure to natural and urban environments', *Journal of Environmental Psychology*, Vol. 11, 1991, pp. 201-230.

van den Berg, A.E., Hartig, T., Staats, H.; 'Preference for Nature in Urbanized Societies: Stress, Restoration, and the Pursuit of Sustainability', *Journal of Social Issues*, Vol. 63, issue 1, 2007, pp. 79-96.

van der Wal, A.J., Schade, H.M., Krabbendam, L., van Vugt, M.; 'Do natural landscapes reduce future discounting in humans?' *Proceedings of the Royal Society - Biological Sciences*, 2013. http://dx.doi.org/10.1098/rspb.2013.2295

Van Hedger, S.C., Nusbaum, H.C., Clohisy, L., Jaeggi, S.M., Bushchkuehl, M., Berman, M.G.; 'Of cricket chirps and car horns: The effect of nature sounds on cognitive performance', *Psychonomic Bulletin & Review*, Vol. 26, 2019, pp. 522-530. https://doi.org/10.3758/s13423-018-1539-1

Wang, D.V., Tsien, J.Z.; 'Convergent processing of both positive and negative motivational signals by the VTA dopamine neuronal populations', *PLoS ONE*, Vol. 6 issue 2, 2011. DOI: 10.1371/journal.pone.0017047

Wang, K., Taylor, R.B.; 'Simulated Walks through Dangerous Alleys: Impacts of Features and Progress on Fear', *Journal of Environmental Psychology*, Vol. 26, 2006, pp. 269-283.

Warm, J.S., Dember, W.N., Parasuraman, R.; 'Effects of olfactory stimulation on performance and stress in visual sustained attention task', *Journal of the Society of Cosmetic Chemists*, 42, 1991, pp. 199-210.

Watts, G., Pheasant, R.J., Horoshenjov, K.V., Ragonesi, L.; 'Measurement and subjective assessment of water generated sounds', *ACTA Acustica United with Acustica*, Vol. 95, 2009 pp. 1032–1039.

Wiener, J.M., Franz, G., Rossmanith, N., Reichelt, A., Mallot, H.A., Bülthoff, H.H.; 'Isovist analysis captures properties of space relevant for locomotion and experience', *Perception*, Vol. 36, 2007, pp. 1066-1083. DOI: 10.1068/p5587

Wigö, H.; 'Technique and human perception of intermittent air velocity variation', KTH Research School, Centre for Built Environment, University of Gavle, 2005.

Windhager, S., Atzwanger, K., Booksteina, F.L, Schaefer, K.; 'Fish in a mall aquarium-an ethological investigation of biophilia', *Landscape and Urban Planning*, Vol. 99, 2011, pp. 23-30.

White, M., Smith, A., Humphryes, K., Pahl, S., Snelling, D., Depledge, M.; 'Blue Space: The Importance of Water for Preference, Affect and Restorativeness Ratings of Natural and Built Scenes', *Journal of Environmental Psychology*, Vol. 30, issue 4, 2010, pp. 482-493.

Yin, J., Zhu, S., MacNaughton, P., Allen, J.A., Spengler, J.D.; 'Physiological and cognitive performance of exposure to biophilic indoor environment', *Building and Environment*, Vol. 132, 2018, pp. 255-262.

Yue, X., Vessel, E.A., Biederman, I.; 'The neural basis of scene preferences', *NeuroReport*, Vol. 18, issue 6, 2007, pp. 525-529.

Zhang, H., Arens, E., Huizenga, C., Han, T.; 'Thermal Sensation and Comfort Models for Non-Uniform and Transient Environments: Part II: Local Comfort of Individual Body Parts', *Building and Environment*, Vol. 45, issue 2, 2010, pp. 389-398.

Zhang, H.; 'Human Thermal Sensation and Comfort in Transient and Non-Uniform Thermal Environments', Ph. D. Thesis, CEDR, University of California at Berkeley, <http://escholarship.org/uc/item/11m0n1wt>, 2003.

D. BIOPHILIC EXPERIENCE
GAP ANALYSIS

Use this table to characterise the current state of a project or design and identify a corrective action or intervention. The contents of the first column can be interchanged with specific space types, biophilic design patterns (Toolkits A and E), desired health outcomes (Toolkit C) or user experiences (Toolkit F), depending on which approach suits the team and where along the project timeline (Toolkit B) the analysis is conducted.

DATE OF ANALYSIS:

PROJECT NAME:

PROJECT OBJECTIVES:

SCOPE OF ANALYSIS: *e.g. room, department, floor, building, campus*

BIOPHILIC DESIGN PRINCIPLE	CURRENT STATE OR EXPERIENCE	TARGET STATE OR EXPERIENCE	CORRECTIVE ACTION/ DESIGN	BIOPHILIC PATTERN(S)	PRIORITY LEVEL	TEAM LEAD	TIMELINE
Repeated and sustained engagement with nature.							
Human adaptations to the natural world that advance health and well-being.							
Emotional attachment to places.							
Positive interactions with nature that encourage an expanded sense of relationship and responsibility for human and natural communities.							
Mutually reinforcing, interconnected and integrative architectural solutions.							

E. HEALTH–TO–COST IMPACT QUADRANT GRID

The quadrant grid (Figure E.1) is a tool for thinking through design options and their potential value to the project in terms of health impact and initial investment impact. As an illustration, Grids 2 and 3 exhibit the range of potential impacts for a sampling of biophilic design features. Use these grids to engage in team discussion or create a new grid, as depicted in Grids 4 and 5, to critique a design feature for allocating budgets that prioritises positive health outcomes.

CONSIDERATIONS

1. The impacts and costs of a biophilic feature are relative to themselves and associated design strategies; therefore, Grids 2 and 3 should not necessarily be used as a primary means to validating one feature over another.

2. Persistent and longer–term health impacts as well as maintenance costs are rarely factored into first-cost investment estimates. When possible, factor in both based on available research and precedents.

3. A biophilic material or product may be cost fungible with the non–biophilic alternative (e.g. finishes).

4. While total cost impact from integrative biophilic design solutions (e.g. water feature integration with building humidity and rainwater management system) may not be known at early stages of a project; potential cost savings should be recorded to inform future decision-making.

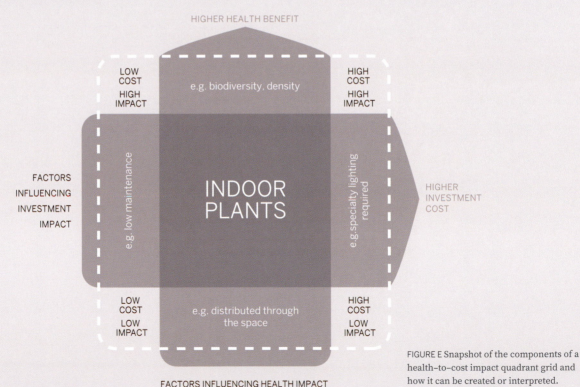

HIGHER HEALTH BENEFIT

LOW COST HIGH IMPACT

e.g. biodiversity, density

HIGH COST HIGH IMPACT

FACTORS INFLUENCING INVESTMENT IMPACT

e.g. low maintenance

INDOOR PLANTS

e.g. specialty lighting required

HIGHER INVESTMENT COST

LOW COST LOW IMPACT

e.g. distributed through the space

HIGH COST LOW IMPACT

FACTORS INFLUENCING HEALTH IMPACT

FIGURE E Snapshot of the components of a health–to–cost impact quadrant grid and how it can be created or interpreted.

HEALTH-TO-COST IMPACT GRID 2
NATURE IN THE SPACE EXPERIENCES

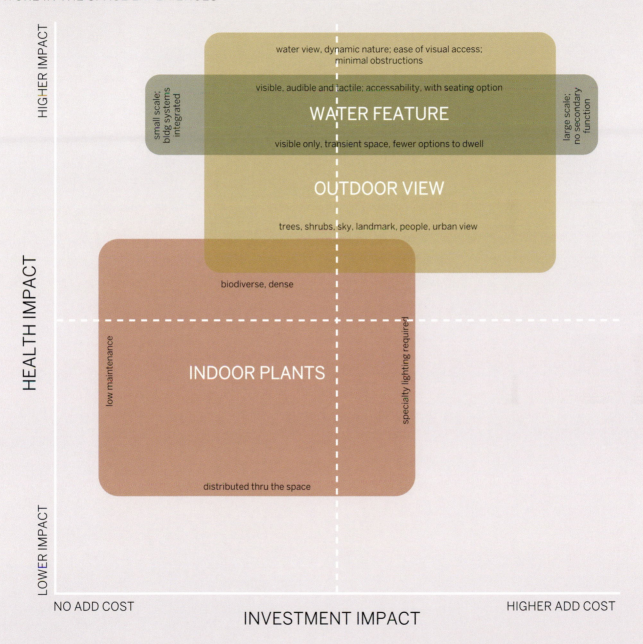

HIGHER IMPACT

LOWER IMPACT

HEALTH IMPACT

water view, dynamic nature; ease of visual access;
minimal obstructions

small scale;
bldg systems
integrated

visible, audible and tactile; accessability, with seating option

large scale;
no secondary
function

WATER FEATURE

visible only, transient space, fewer options to dwell

OUTDOOR VIEW

trees, shrubs, sky, landmark, people, urban view

biodiverse, dense

low maintenance

INDOOR PLANTS

specialty lighting required

distributed thru the space

NO ADD COST

HIGHER ADD COST

INVESTMENT IMPACT

HEALTH-TO-COST IMPACT GRID 3
NATURAL ANALOGUES AND SPATIAL EXPERIENCES

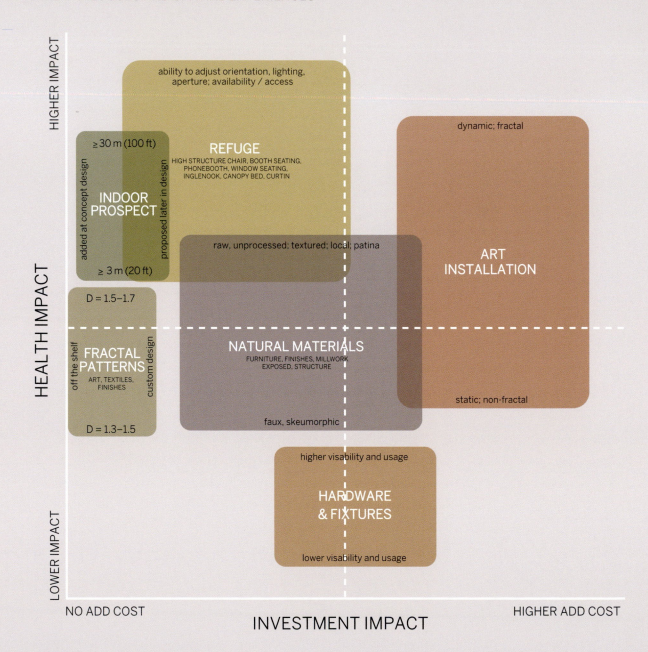

HIGHER IMPACT

HEALTH IMPACT

LOWER IMPACT

ability to adjust orientation, lighting, aperture; availability / access

≥ 30 m (100 ft)

added at concept design

proposed later in design

REFUGE
HIGH STRUCTURE CHAIR, BOOTH SEATING, PHONEBOOTH, WINDOW SEATING, INGLENOOK, CANOPY BED, CURTIN

INDOOR PROSPECT

≥ 3 m (20 ft)

dynamic; fractal

ART INSTALLATION

raw, unprocessed; textured; local; patina

D = 1.5–1.7

off the shelf

custom design

FRACTAL PATTERNS
ART, TEXTILES, FINISHES

NATURAL MATERIALS
FURNITURE, FINISHES, MILLWORK EXPOSED, STRUCTURE

static; non-fractal

D = 1.3–1.5

faux, skeumorphic

higher visability and usage

HARDWARE & FIXTURES

lower visability and usage

NO ADD COST

INVESTMENT IMPACT

HIGHER ADD COST

HEALTH-TO-COST IMPACT
GRID 4 WORKSHEET SAMPLE

Health outcomes and investment costs for planning and design characteristics can be organised by scale of impact. Each grid quadrant presents a scenario for conceptualising the potential value of a biophilic design strategy. Refer to Grids 2 and 3 as well as the Health Outcomes Chart (Toolkit C) for design factors that may inform health and investment impacts for a particular design feature. Create your own possible design scenarios for each quadrant. Consider which scenario offers the best value proposition.

Refer to Grids 2 and 3 as well as the Health Outcomes Chart (Toolkit C) for design factors that may inform health and investment impacts for a particular design feature. Create your own possible design scenarios for each quadrant. Consider which scenario offers the best value proposition.

BIOPHILIC DESIGN FEATURE:

Water feature

HIGH HEALTH IMPACT FACTORS: *engages multiple senses; paired with seating option(s); accessible to many people most of the time*

LOW COST IMPACT FACTORS: *small scale building or site systems integrated*

HIGH COST IMPACT FACTORS: *large scale; no secondary function*

HIGHER HEALTH IMPACT LOWER/NO ADD COST	HIGHER HEALTH IMPACT HIGHER ADD COST
SENARIO A: *engages all senses; multiple seating options; medium scale; integrated with workplace noise distration mitigation strategy*	SENARIO B: *engages visual + aural senses; available to many people from more than one zone; has seating options; is large scale*
SENARIO C: *mostly engages visual sense only; motor is audible; small desktop feature in lounge area*	SENARIO D: *located in lobby; only visible in lobby; has a seating option facing away from it; large scale*
LOWER HEALTH IMPACT LOWER/NO ADD COST	LOWER HEALTH IMPACT HIGHER ADD COST

LOW HEALTH IMPACT FACTORS: *does not engage tactile or aural senses (only visual); in a transient space with fewer options to dwell*

251

F. USER EXPERIENCE WORKSHEETS

No project has an unlimited budget for biophilic design. This series of worksheets is intended to help focus on the experiential needs of different user groups and to then identify the most effective biophilic design patterns and interventions. In the following steps, identify user groups and potential stressors (i.e. experiences or situations that induce stress for that user group). On a floor plan, overlay anticipated pedestrian routes and spaces to be occupied by each of those users, and then identify the areas/zones in which multiple user types experience stress, need cognitive focus or would benefit from mood enhancement. These are the areas that should then be targeted for biophilic design interventions.

Refer to the Health Outcomes Chart (Toolkit C) or Gap Analysis (Toolkit D), if one has been conducted for your project. These tools can be found in the Nature Inside Biophilic Design Toolkit.

STEP 1.
USER TYPE PROFILE

MATERIALS NEEDED
Input or feedback from owner on projected or actual end users.

TASK
Identify primary user types or groups, their priorities, potential peeves and stress points. Add additional users as appropriate.

USER TYPE: *Family travelling with young children*

USER PRIORITIES AND PEEVES: *In an airport there are a number of locations that can cause stress for this type of traveller. Corralling children and luggage at the check-in and baggage drop-off points can be a major juggling act. Keeping the kids calm in the security queue can be an issue, along with the process of then reassembling the clothing and the contents of carry-ons in the recomposure area. A stop at a play area while waiting to board the plane is an opportunity to decompress.*

STEP 2.
'DAY IN THE LIFE' SEQUENCE OF ACTIVITIES

MATERIALS NEEDED
Floor plan, trace (optional), coloured markers (one colour or line pattern per user type).

TASK
Conduct a two-dimensional walk-through of the space or place for each user type, asking what is the first thing they each do upon entering, how their day unfolds, what key activities they engage in (e.g. coffee breaks, meetings, watching television, lunch, shopping) and how long they might dwell in each place.

OUTCOME
Understanding of how each user might flow through the space and where paths overlap the most with other users. These overlaps indicate tentative priority spots for biophilic design interventions. Additional value if population density or dwell time can be overlaid.

STEP 3.
EXPERIENTIAL MAPPING

MATERIALS NEEDED
Annotated floor plan from Step 2.

TASK
Consider how a user group's profession, age, gender, culture or religion, physical and sensory differences may each influence where and how stress may be experienced in that sequence. Annotate the floor plan or create a matrix (y = user, x = activity/space) to map out existing or desired experiences, both stress-inducing and positive experiences. Use words, colour or another method to indicate degree of experiential impact the space has, or needs to have, on the user.

USER TYPE	ARRIVAL	CHECK-IN	BATHROOM	SECURITY	SHOPPING	BOARDING
Business traveler	low	low	low	low	low	medium
Sports team	medium	medium	low	medium	low	medium
Elderly person	high	high	medium	high	medium	high

EXAMPLE MATRIX: AIRPORT STRESS

OUTCOME
This exercise should begin to reveal which user experiences occur in the same places, as well as which zones or interstitial spaces could offer positive experiences that might typically be overlooked. Broad matrix content may be useful for explaining concepts or concerns to clients and collaborators; while detailed content may be useful for design team members charged with translating targeted experiences into effective design solutions.

STEP 4.
USER EXPERIENCE
AND SPACE TYPE PRIORITISATION

MATERIALS NEEDED
Annotated floor plans and/or matrix from Steps 2 and 3.

TASK
Use the annotated floor plans and/or matrices from Steps 2 and 3 to synthesise common threads between user type activity and health impact experience. Select specific places where the overlaps appear to have the greatest potential impact – based on highest foot traffic, dwell times and type of experience. Include secondary spaces that may demand a unique user experience.

OUTCOME
Focused understanding of spaces or places for mitigating stress and enhancing user experience. Identifying priority spaces for biophilic design interventions may also help to rationalise greater 'biophilic intensity' (i.e. where to focus the effort, where to spend your money).

EXAMPLE MATRIX: AIRPORT			
SPACE TYPE	EXPERIENCE	DESIRED HEALTH OUTCOME	IMPACT PRIORITY
Security screening	10–20 min; 90% of users experience stress	Reduce stress	high
Secondary stairway	1 min; foot traffic is <50 people/day; no windows	Visual comfort	low
Bathrooms	5–10 min; high traffic, tends to have a large impact on users' overall perception of airport experience	Improved perceptions	medium

STEP 5.
BIOPHILIC DESIGN SOLUTIONS MATRIX

MATERIALS NEEDED

Analysis from Step 4; health outcomes matrix (see Toolkit C) or list of biophilic design patterns (see Toolkit A); user profiles (from Step 1) and annotated floor plans (Step 2) may also be helpful.

TASK

Using the analysis from Step 4, describe the high priority space types — programming, desired user experience, existing attributes that could be leveraged and the design goal, problem and/or opportunity. Then, use the health outcomes matrix, or a similar reference, to identify biophilic design patterns that could support the desired experience and health outcomes. Next, identify a series of potential design interventions for each space type relative to potential cost and health impact.

EXAMPLE SPACE TYPE: FOOD SPOTS	
DESCRIPTION	DESIGN SOLUTIONS BY COST
- *Cafeterias, kitchenettes, cafes, hydration stations and baristas serve as community anchors on our campus. Our design intent is to provide convivial spots that connect employees to food and place.* - *Existing architectural geometries and fenestration cannot be altered but fit-out standards are currently undefined, giving room for innovative experiential opportunities, materials palette, lighting and seating.*	NEUTRAL COST DESIGN SOLUTIONS - *Use a colour palette that reflects prominent regional foods* - *Outdoor picnic tables are shaded by trees* LOW OR MODERATE COST DESIGN SOLUTIONS - *Indoor booth seating* - *Employee vegetable and herb garden* HIGHER FIRST COST STRATEGIES WITH GREATER IMPACT ON HEALTH, BRAND, REVENUE OR OTHER ANCILLARY BENEFIT(S) - *Water feature with plants and seating around it*
PATTERNS AND CHARACTERISTICS	
Colour, refuge, variety of seating options, physical connection with nature, water	

G. SYNERGIES WITH STANDARDS AND RATING SYSTEMS

Design certification standards (e.g. BREEAM, LEED, WELL, LBC) have become a benchmark for the way a project is developed. Architects and planners often use these standards to set project goals and then later leverage the certification requirements to justify retaining green and wellness-promoting design features. By identifying the biophilic design opportunities that support green building requirements, designers can better justify their relative importance to a project.

Whether it is explicitly stated or not, most rating systems provide ample opportunity for incorporating biophilic design into the building design and construction process. Some rating systems are direct proponents of biophilic design with prescriptive requirements for use of biophilic design strategies in and around a building. Others indirectly promote the use of biophilic design with performance-based measures for supporting occupant health and wellness (e.g. access to daylighting and views, outdoor recreation and relaxation space).

The following table identifies key credits and certification requirements that overlap with biophilic design strategies. Those in bold are credits that directly promote the use of biophilic design. Although non-exhaustive, the table helps to illuminate the plentiful opportunities to incorporate biophilic design to the benefit of not just the occupant, but also the client through the certifications they can attain.

BALANCING PRIORITIES: BIOPHILIC GOODS AND GREEN RATING SYSTEMS

Material toxicity and carbon footprints are hot topics in the industry. While a full chain of custody documentation is gaining momentum, soft goods and furniture options are still limited in terms of what qualifies as being both biophilic and either red-list free, regionally sourced or carbon footprint minimising. Options

are further diminished when pursuing green building certification such as from BREEAM®, the WELL Building Standard® or the Living Building Challenge℠, each of which directly or indirectly call for biophilic design. The table details how biophilic design is approached in some of the frequently pursued rating systems and standards. See the Phipps Conservatory (Case Study 11.2) as an example of a biophilic project pursuing several rating systems simultaneously.

When commitment to the pursuit of a rating system comes late in the design process, an upheaval to the design often results, which can directly impact the biophilic design strategy, particularly when design interventions have been confined to soft goods. For instance, full chain of custody for red-list free products may be easier to obtain for commercial projects than for residential projects, but will probably require rethinking at least several products and materials. For 250 West 57th Street (see Case Study 7.2), the commitment to pursue WELL certification came late enough in the design process that the interior design had to be significantly re-engineered; the soft goods in particular were directly impacted. Options for textiles and furniture that met expectations for aesthetics and natural materials became more difficult to find.

Hitting multiple goals with a single product can be a daunting task. A comprehensive biophilic strategy — i.e. not limited to soft goods — helps to minimise degradation of the intended experiential impact caused by substituting out a biophilic product due to non-compliance with green building certification requirements.

With the widespread growth in green building and awareness of public mental and physiological health, the challenges of aligning client goals with rating systems requirements and biophilic design ideologies are likely to fade away over time.

STANDARD	SNAPSHOT	BIOPHILIA ENTRY POINTS
BREEAM 2018 3.0	The Building Research Establishment Environmental Assessment Method (BREEAM) is a sustainability rating system for the performance of the built environment. BREEAM addresses biophilic design primarily in the Health & Wellbeing (HEA) section of the rating system, although opportunities to gain credit through particular biophilic design patterns can also be found in the Land Use & Ecology (LE) section.	As of this printing, BREEAM is exploring the possibility of offering credit for projects that 'include nature and aspects of nature in the building and its surroundings to reconnect people with nature in order to reduce stress, enhance creativity and clarity of thought and improve our well-being'. In the meantime, these credits indirectly address biophilic design: HEA 01: Visual Comfort HEA 07: Safe and Healthy Surroundings LE 04: Ecological Change and Enhancement
ECODISTRICTS V1.3	Ecodistricts is a rating system meant to encourage sustainable development at the neighbourhood and district scale. The Ecodistricts Standard promotes the use of biophilic design across several of the 'Priorities', most notably in Priority #6: Living Infrastructure.	Priority #1 Place: Culture + Identity Public Spaces Priority #3 Health + Wellbeing: Health Priority #6 Living Infrastructure: Connection with Nature and Natural Features
ENVISION V3	As a sustainability rating system focused on infrastructure, ENVISION addresses biophilic design in the Quality of Life (QL) section by incentivising infrastructure that maintains local character and enhances public spaces.	QL1.1 Improve Community Quality of Life QL3.2 Preserve Historic & Cultural Resources QL3.3 Enhance Views and Local Character QL3.3 Enhance Public Spaces & Amenities

FITWEL V2.1	As a rating system for buildings and communities focused on promoting public health, at least three of the 12 Fitwel Strategies support biophilic design, including for outdoor spaces, workspaces, dwellings and shared spaces. Specific strategies vary slightly depending on the building project type.	Strategy 3: Outdoor Spaces
		   Proximity to Outdoor Space and Amenities
		   Walking Trail
		   Restorative Garden; Fruit/vegetable Garden
		
		Strategy 7: Workspaces/Dwellings
		   Natural Daylighting
		   Views of Nature
		
		Strategy 8: Shared Spaces
		   Quiet Room

GREEN STAR V1.3	Green Star is a sustainability rating system for the design and operation of buildings and communities. Biophilic design is primarily addressed in the Indoor Environmental Quality section of the standard.	Indoor Air Quality: 9.2C Natural Ventilation Acoustic Comfort: 10.1 Internal Noise Levels Visual Comfort: 12.0 Glare Reduction Visual Comfort: 12.1 Daylighting Visual Comfort: 12.2 Views Life Cycle Impacts: 19B.4: Structural Timber Responsible Building Materials: 20.2 Timber Ecological Value: 23.1: Ecological Value Indoor Pollutants 12.3 Indoor Plants

STANDARD	SNAPSHOT	BIOPHILIA ENTRY POINTS
LEED V4.1	Leadership for Energy and Environmental Design (LEED) is a sustainability rating system for the performance of the built environment. Biophilic design is directly addressed in the innovation (ID) section of the rating system. Biophilic design strategies can also contribute to several Indoor Environmental Quality (EQ), Materials and Resources (MR) and Sustainable Sites (SS) credits.	**EQpc123: Designing with Nature, Biophilic Design for the Indoor Environment** This credit incentivises the development and implementation of a biophilic design plan using at least five distinct design strategies. Each design strategy should provide quantifiable metrics where possible and describe reasoning and relevant research. SS: Open Space SS: Protect or Restore Habitat MR: Building Product Disclosure and Optimization MRpc102: Legal Wood EQ: Enhanced Indoor Air Quality Strategies EQ: Interior Lighting EQ: Daylight EQ: Quality Views EQ: Acoustic Performance
LBC V4.0	The Living Building Challenge[SM] (LBC) and Living Community Challenge (LCC) are sustainability rating systems for the performance of the built environment. LBC has long upheld biophilic design as an essential component to regenerative building design and performance. Biophilic design is primarily addressed in the Beauty petal of the rating system, although several petals, including Place, and Health + Happiness petals support particular elements of biophilic design.	**Beauty 19: Beauty + Biophilia** As a core imperative, this credit mandates the 'incorporation of meaningful biophilic design elements into the project'. Beginning as a one–day exploration of biophilic design opportunities, project teams must eventually develop a biophilic design framework and implementation plan. Place 01: Ecology of Place Health + Happiness 09: Healthy Interior Environment Health + Happiness 10: Healthy Interior Performance Health + Happiness 11: Access to Nature
RELi V2.0	RELi is a rating system emphasising the use of resilient design principles in community, building and infrastructure projects. The RELi system addresses biophilic design primarily in the Productivity, Health & Diversity (PH) section. Secondary opportunities to gain credit through the use of particular biophilic design patterns can be found in the Panoramic Approach section (PA), Community Cohesion, Social & Economic Vitality section (CV), as well as the Hazard Adaptation & Mitigation (HA) section.	PAc7.0: Study + Living Design for Advanced Resilience Using a Diversity of Ecological–based Perspectives PHc1.0: Human HDP: Expanded IAQ, Daylight & Views, Fresh Air CVr1: Improve Common Quality of Life CVc1: Incorporate Important Community Views & Aspects of Local Landscape HAc3: Passive Thermal Safety, Thermal Comfort & Lighting Design Strategies

STANDARD	SNAPSHOT	BIOPHILIA ENTRY POINTS
SITES V2.0	The Sustainable SITES Initiative® (SITES) focuses exclusively on the environmental performance of the landscape, including impacts to human health. One of SITES' guiding principles is to 'design with culture and nature'. The SITES system addresses biophilic design in Section 6: Human Health + Wellbeing (HHWB).	HHWB 6.1: Protect and Maintain Cultural and Historic Places HHWB 6.3: Support Mental Restoration HHWB 6.6: Support Social Connection Water 3.5: Design Functional Stormwater Features as Amenities Soil+Veg 4.10: Use Vegetation to Minimise Building Energy Use Materials 5.6: Use Regional Materials
WELL V2	The WELL Building Standard™ (WELL) focuses exclusively on promoting the health and well-being of the people in buildings and communities. Biophilic design is one of many features identified as methods for supporting mental health. Biophilic design is primarily addressed in the Mind section of the standard, although several categories, including Air, Light, Thermal Comfort and Sound, grant opportunities to use particular biophilic design patterns.	**Mind 02: Access to Nature** This feature encourages the use of biophilic design indoors and outdoors to support occupant well-being. It requires that indoor environments include direct connection to nature through views or indoor natural features (water, plants, light), indirect connection to nature through natural materials or images, and spatial layouts that use environmental psychology to enhance experience. **Mind 09: Enhanced Access to Nature** This feature goes beyond Mind 02: Access to Nature by providing prescriptive numerical benchmarks for the integration of natural environments indoors and outdoors. For example, it specifies that at least 75% of workspaces have a direct line of sight to indoor plants and or water features. Air 07: Operable Windows Light 05: Enhanced Daylight Access Light 03: Circadian Light Design Thermal Comfort 03: Thermal Zoning Sound 05: Sound Masking Mind 07: Restorative Spaces

H. ENTRY POINTS FOR TEAM ENGAGEMENT

Each discipline has something valuable to offer a project in order to bring nature inside buildings and to connect building occupants with nature. The goal of this worksheet is to help establish clarity about stakeholder entry points and opportunities in the context of a biophilic design agenda.

At the beginning of a project, consider how different disciplines may be able to contribute to the concept, design and success of a biophilic design strategy. Consider what perspectives each discipline can bring to the table, how collaborative roles are to be communicated and maintained, and when to engage them during the design process. Refer to the list of team disciplines as well as sections A–G of the Toolkit to help guide the discussion.

TABLE H. Project team entry points for biophilic design

DISCIPLINE	PERSPECTIVE OR RESPONSIBILITY BROUGHT TO BIOPHILIC DESIGN DISCUSSION	ENGAGEMENT TIMELINE
Acoustician / Sound Artist	*auditory experience and perception of sound in space (psychoacoustics); nature–based alternatives to noise masking; place–making*	*Schematic Design; Design Development*
Commissioning Agent	*integration of biophilic design parameters into Owner Project Requirements*	*Schematic Design; Construction Administration*
Sustainability Manager or Consultant	*aligning biophilic design goals with other sustainability initiatives*	*Periodically, from Concept through Design Development*
Discipline:		
Discipline:		
Discipline:		

TEAM DISCIPLINES TO ENGAGE IN A BIOPHILIC DESIGN EFFORT

DESIGN TEAM

– Acoustician / Sound Artist
– Architect
– Commissioning Agent
– Contractor
– Decorator
– Engineer: MEP
– Engineer: Civil, Environmental
– Environmental Graphic Design
– Envelope Consultant
– Thematic Environments Designer
– Interior Designer
– Lighting Designer
– Landscape Architect
– Miller / Craftsman
– Sustainability Manager / Consultant

OWNER / OCCUPANT TEAM

– Client / Owner / Executives
– Human Resources / Talent Acquisition & Management
– Facility Manager: Engineering, Maintenance
– Facility Manager: Landscape, Maintenance
– Real Estate Professional
– User / Future Occupant

SUBJECT MATTER EXPERTS

– Environmental Psychologist / Neuroscientist
– Biologist, Ecologist, Botanist
– Urban Designer
– Community Planner
– Artist
– City Agency: Planning / Neighbourhoods / Sustainability / Transportation / Utilities

VENDOR AND PRODUCT SALES

– Building Product Manufacturer
– Sales Representative

I. ESSENTIAL READINGS

There are hundreds of publications available. This list represents a handful of the foundational theories and research known for addressing key issues on the connection between health, nature and the built environment.

BOOKS

Timothy Beatley, *Handbook of Biophilic City Planning & Design*, Island Press, Washington DC, 2017.

Stephen R. Kellert, *Building for Life: Designing and understanding the human-nature connection*, Island Press, Washington, DC, 2005.

Stephen R. Kellert, Judith H. Heerwagen & Martin Mador, *Biophilic Design: The Theory, Science and Practice of Bringing Buildings to Life* (especially Ch. 1, 6, 22, 23), Wiley, 2008.

Stephen R. Kellert and Edward & O. Wilson, *Biophilia Hypothesis* (especially Ch. 1–4, 15), Shearwater, 1995.

Grant Hildebrant, *The Wright Space: Pattern and Meaning in Frank Lloyd Wright's Houses*, University of Washington Press, 1991.

Richard Louv, *The Nature Principle: Reconnecting with Life in a Virtual Age*, Algonquin Books, 2012.

Amanda Sturgeon, *Creating Biophilic Buildings,* Ecotone Publishing, 2017.

Florence Williams, *The Nature Fix: Why Nature Makes Us Happier, Healthier, and More Creative*, W. W. Norton & Company, 2018.

Edward O. Wilson, *Biophilia*, Harvard University Press, Cambridge, MA, 1984.

WHITE PAPERS AND REPORTS

William D. Browning, Catherine O. Ryan, Joseph O. Clancy, *'14 Patterns of Biophilic Design: Improving health and wellbeing in the built environment'*, New York, Terrapin Bright Green, 2014.

William D. Browning & Dakota Walker, *'An Ear for Nature: Psychoacoustic strategies for workplace distraction and the bottom line'*, New York, Terrapin Bright Green, 2018.

William D. Browning, Rebecca Macies, Catherine O. Ryan, Lorraine Francis, Lili Fisher, *'Human Spaces 2.0: Biophilic Design in Hospitality'*, Interface Inc., 2017.

Sir Cary Cooper and Bill Browning, *'Human Spaces: The Global Impact of Biophilic Design in the Workplace'*, Interface Inc., 2015.

Jim Determan, Mary Anne Akers, Tom Albright, Bill Browning, Catherine Martin-Dunlop, Paul Archibald, Valerie Caruolo, *'The Impact of Biophilic Learning Spaces on Student Success'*, AIA Upjohn Research Initiative, 2019.

Lisa Heschong, *Thermal Delight in Architecture,* Cambridge, MA: MIT Press, 1979.

Lisa Heschong, *'Windows and Offices: A Study of Office Worker Performance and the Indoor Environment'*, Technical Report, California Energy Commission, 2003, P500-03-082-A-9.

Paula Melton, Brent Ehrlich, Nadav Malin, Candace Pearson, Alex Wilson (eds), *'How to Access the Full Power of Biophilia'*, Spotlight Report, BuildingGreen Inc., 2019.

Stephen R. Kellert & Elizabeth F. Calabrese, *'The practice of biophilic design'*, 2015, https://www.biophilic-design.com/.

Dakota Walker, Catherine O. Ryan, William D. Browning, Rebecca Macies, *'The Economics of Biophilia: Why designing with nature in mind makes financial sense'*, New York, Terrapin Bright Green, Second edition, 2020.

JOURNAL ARTICLES

Rachel Kaplan & Stephen Kaplan, *The Experience of Nature: A Psychological Perspective*, Cambridge: Cambridge University Press, 1989.

Kate E. Lee, Kathryn J.H. Williams, Leisa D. Sargent, Nicholas S.G. Williams, Katherine A. Johnson, '40-second green roof views sustain attention: The role of micro-breaks in attention restoration', *Journal of Environmental Psychology*, 42, 2015, 182–189.

Richard Louv, 'Do our kids have nature-deficit disorder', *Health and Learning*, 67 (4), 2009, pp. 24–30.

Peter H. Kahn, Jr., Batya Friedman, Brian Gill, Jennifer Hagman, Rachel L. Severson, Nathan G. Freier, Erika N. Feldman, Sybil Carrere, Anna Stolyare, 'A Plasma Display Window? The Shifting Baseline Problem in a Technology Mediated Natural World', *Journal of Environmental Psychology*, 28, 2008, pp. 192–199.

Gordon H. Orians & Judith H. Heerwagen, 'Evolved Responses to Landscapes. In J.H. Barkow, L. Cosmides, & J. Tooby (Eds), *The Adapted Mind: Evolutionary Psychology and the Generation of Culture.* New York, NY: Oxford University Press, 1992, pp. 555–579.

Bum-Jin Park, Yuko Tsunetsugu, Tamami Kasetani, Takeshi Morikawa, Takahide Kagawa, 'Physiological Effects of Forest Recreation in a Young Conifer Forest in Hinokage Town, Japan', *Silva Fennica*, 43(2), 2009, pp. 291–301.

Catherine Ryan-Balagtas, 'Actions for Elevating the Experience of Architecture: A Design Challenge of the 21st Century', *New Design Ideas*, 3 (2), 2019, pp. 164–168.

Catherine O. Ryan and William D. Browning, 'Biophilic Design', R.A. Meyers (ed.), *Encyclopedia of Sustainability Science and Technology*, Springer, 2018.

Catherine O. Ryan, William D. Browning, Joseph O. Clancy, Scott L. Andrews, Namita B. Kallianpurkar, 'Biophilic Design Patterns: Emerging Nature-Based Parameters for Health and Well-Being in the Built Environment', *Archnet International Journal of Architectural Research*, 8 (2), 2014, pp. 62–76.

Roger S. Ulrich, 'View through a window may influence recovery from surgery', *Science*, 224, 1984.

Roger S. Ulrich, Lennart Bogren, Stuart K. Gardiner, Stefan Lundine, 'Psychiatric ward design can reduce aggressive behaviour', *Journal of Environmental Psychology*, 57, 2018, pp. 53–66.

Jie Yin, Nastaran Arfaei, Piers MacNaughton, Paul J. Catalano, Joseph G. Allen, John D. Spengler, 'Effects of biophilic interventions in office on stress reaction and cognitive function: A randomized crossover study in virtual reality', *Indoor Air*, 29, 2019, pp. 1028–1039.

OTHER RESOURCES

Stephen R. Kellert and Bill Finnegan, *Biophilic Design: The Architecture of Life*, Bullfrog Films, 2009, (Video trailer available)

J. GLOSSARY OF TERMS

Understanding key concepts and theories behind biophilic design can make practical application easier to identify and rationalise. The following cross-disciplinary terms are defined and then related to the practice of biophilic design.

Affordance theory. Coined by American psychologist James J. Gibson (1904–1979), affordances are what the environment offers as visually perceived by the individual.[1] Affordance theory states that the world is perceived not only in terms of object shapes and spatial relationships but also in terms of object possibilities for action, i.e. affordances' — perception drives action: the affordance is a chair, the action is to sit. Research on 'embodied cognition' grounds all symbolic activity in the experiences of the body. Research by Zakaria Djebbara and others begins to set the groundwork on how spatial conditions subconsciously signal possible behaviours with a specific space.[2]

Alliesthesia. Also referred to as 'thermal delight', alliesthesia was first introduced in 1992 by French physiologist Michel Cabanac.[3] There are two types of alliesthesia, temporal and spatial, which can be experienced as sensory stimuli (thermal/haptic, visual/optic, auditory, gustatory, olfactory). In the built environment, alliesthesia manifests as a conditioning of people, particularly their feet and hands, rather than of an entire space. Gail Brager frames the design challenge as the ability to determine how 'uncomfortable' an occupant needs to be before thermal delight is introduced,[4] and then in what form such delight is proffered (e.g. wood versus metal table top; operable window). Diffuse and Dynamic Light, Material Connection with Nature and Thermal and Airflow Variability are the most directly relatable biophilic design patterns. Alliesthesia should not be confused with the neurological disorder allesthesia.

Attention restoration theory. Posits that when experiencing nature, the prefrontal cortex quiets down and the brain uses less energy to process what it is experiencing,[5] after which cognitive capacity is improved. It takes about 40 seconds of viewing nature for this shift to occur within the brain.[6] See also **soft fascination.**

Authenticity. A condition perceived as being real and not a facsimile. Also expressed as a desire to identify and live amongst that which is true and genuine. See also **greenwash** and **skeuomorphism** for greater context.

Biophilia. German psychoanalyst Erich Fromm (1900–1980) first coined the term biophilia and, in 1964, defined it as 'the connections that human beings subconsciously seek with the rest of life',[7] and in 1973 as 'the passionate love of life and of all that is alive'.[8] Harvard biologist Edward O. Wilson (1929–) later popularised the term in his 1984 publication in which he defined biophilia as the 'innate tendency to focus on life and life-like processes',[9] and then again in 1993 he defined biophilia as both 'a complex behavior' and the 'innately emotional affiliation of human beings to other living organisms'.[10] Countless variations of these early definitions are used today, all directly or indirectly relating nature to humankind's mental and physical health and well-being.

Biophilia hypothesis. Harvard biologist Edward O. Wilson (1929–) introduced the hypothesis in 1984 and then published on the topic in 1993 with Stephen R. Kellert, positing that an instinctive bond exists between human beings and other living beings and systems. The intent of establishing a hypothesis, Kellert explains, was to be cautious not to 'promote a romantic idealization of nature'[11] and to fuel, as it so happens, much of the scientific research that has mounted in the recent decades.

Biophilic design. Design that intentionally connects humans with direct or indirect experiences of nature within the built environment. **Parameters** of biophilic design are qualitative or quantitative metrics, the latter of which is often desired for the convenience of fitting into contemporary architecture and engineering practices. Qualitative parameters (e.g. access to daylight and outdoors) can be particularly useful for site selection and experiential design. **Patterns** of biophilic design are typically articulated as either experiences or characteristics of nature. This book uses the 15 patterns developed by Terrapin Bright Green, which are grounded in science-supported connections between nature, neuroscience and the built environment. **Principles** of biophilic design are 'fundamental conditions for the effective practice of biophilic design',[12] communicating a vision of health and well-being in symbiosis with nature. The Principles support an adaptable methodology for realising that vision. See the Introduction for more on Patterns and Chapter 2 for more on the Principles.

Biophilic urban acupuncture. Finnish architect Marco Casagrande (1971–) defines urban acupuncture as a socio-environmental theory that combines sociology and urban design with acupuncture, a theory of traditional Chinese medicine, whereby 'tactical, small-scale interventions on the urban fabric' aim to have 'ripple effects and transformation on the larger urban organism... to relieve stress and industrial tension in the urban environment'.[13] Biophilic urban acupuncture specifically targets human health and well-being as a desired outcome of these tactical interventions.

Biophobia. A fear of or aversion to nature or living things. While biophobia is arguably genetic, to a degree, it is also a learnt response mechanism through direct experience, culture and education, which can include architectural education.[14] The most common biophobic responses are to spiders, snakes, predators, blood and heights — elements that either directly threaten or signal danger through humanity's evolutionary path. When tempered with an element of safety (e.g. railing or glass window), however, the experience can be transformed into one of curiosity, exhilaration and even a type of mind-body systems recalibration.

Circadian-effective light. Having ample daylighting alone does not necessarily ensure optimal impact on the occupants' circadian rhythm (a daily cycle of naturally-occurring biological changes). Circadian-effective lighting design considers the amount of light falling on the eye, spectrum/wavelength of light, and timing and duration of exposure. These factors influence sleepiness, alertness, vitality and energy over the course of a day — strong reasons for why circadian-effective light is often a design priority for workplaces and schools. While there is continued industry debate over the best metric for measuring circadian-effective light, there is some consensus on effective lighting design strategies and health outcomes.

Ecological aesthetic theory. The ecological aesthetic theory proclaims that knowledge about the ecological functions of a landscape will increase preference ratings for that landscape. This theory depends on knowledge as a key driver of landscape preference.[15] As a cultural theory, it can somewhat explain the variations in landscape preferences between social classes. For instance, college students are reported to have more favourable attitudes towards wilderness than secondary school students.[16] Preferences for more tamed landscapes, typical of heavily urbanised environments, by lower income groups, is contrasted by the preference for wilder landscapes by higher income groups; it can be deduced that education, more accessible to those with higher socioeconomic status, plays a key role in developing the ecological aesthetic.[17]

Ecophobia. An unreasonable but deeply conditioned disgust for or reaction against natural forms or places. A learnt response mechanism through direct experience, culture and education, which can include architectural education.[18]

Environmental generational amnesia. The shifting baseline for what is considered a normal environmental condition as it continues to degrade. As environmental degradation continues, the baseline continues to shift with each ensuing generation, each perceiving the current degraded condition as the norm or non-degraded condition.[19] This shifting baseline varies across cultures, geographic regions and sub-groups,[20] influencing environmental stewardship, proximity and access to nature and the biophilic experience. Helping a community to understand what their home looked like when it was a healthy, intact ecosystem is one way of making a Connection with Natural Systems and potentially also help to foster interest in restoring environmental conditions.

Fractals. A geometric object or shape which exhibits self-similarity across scales. A **fractal dimension** is a general measure — an integer quantity or fractional value — of how quickly length, area or volume change with decreasing scale. **Exact** fractals, also known as **classical**, **linear** or **regular**, are self-repeating patterns, with corresponding increase or reduction in size; exact fractals are mathematical and can be highly appealing, but do not appear in nature. **Statistical** or **natural** fractals show the same statistical properties at different scales, yet appearing organic and random. Familiar natural phenomena with statistical fractal features include trees, snowflakes and frost crystals, ferns, pineapples, river networks, clouds, lightning and the dappled light under trees. Over time, humans have adapted to more easily, efficiently and fluidly process naturally-occurring fractal patterns. This adaptation is known as the **fractal fluency**

theory. The visual stimuli provided by fractal patterns can vary in complexity, having a range of experiential outcomes for the observer. Subsequently, fractals are a popular focus of biophilic design application and research.

Greenwash. A marketing strategy in which green or sustainable characteristics are deceptively used to promote a positive perception or higher value of a product, material or activity. Biophilic design strategies implemented without consideration of health impact, but marketed as such, would be considered greenwashing. A classic example is a large green wall in an office lobby that cannot be experienced from elsewhere in the building, but is featured in an advertisement for a healthy workplace.

Nature–deficit disorder. Coined by American author Richard Louv in 2005, nature-deficit disorder is a non-medical descriptor for 'the human costs of alienation from nature', largely rooted in the idea that as humans spend less and less time outdoors, mental health and behavioural problems arise, especially among children.[21]

Neurobiophilia. First coined by American biologist Tierney Thys in 2014, neurobiophilia is 'a subdiscipline of neuroscience that explores how functions and dynamics of the human brain respond to nature'.[22] Routed in the biophilia hypothesis, research in neurobiophilia 'examines both the cognitive benefits of nature contact and the neurological impacts of nature deprivation…' and how to alleviate such deleterious mental effects in the built environment, particularly in extreme environments such as prisons and research stations in Antarctica and outer space.

Parallax. The effect whereby the position or direction of an object appears to differ when viewed from different positions. Parallax arises with a change in viewpoint occurring due to motion of the observer, of the observed, or of both, such as experienced when driving past an orchard or vineyard. The human brain exploits the parallax to gain depth perception and estimate distances to objects.

Prospect–refuge theory. British geographer Jay Appleton (1919–2015) proposed and advanced the notion of 'prospect-refuge' in his many publications. As a theory, certain environments are believed to meet basic human psychological needs by feeling both secure (from physical or environmental threat) and connected (to people, place and/or activity) — in other words, 'the capacity to observe (prospect) without being exposed (refuge)'.[23] This theory was popularised in architecture beginning in the 1990s, and is the focus of American architect and architectural historian Grant Hildebrand's (1934–) book in which he closely critiques the architecture of Frank Lloyd Wright. In biophilic design, prospect and refuge are perhaps two of the most commonly utilised patterns; the design challenge is often in finding the right balance between the two for the project and its occupants.

Psychoacoustics. The science of sound perception. The peripheral auditory system, responsible for capturing sound, is needed to hear something, but human perception of a sound is based on sound spectrum and volume level as well as the meaning we attach to that sound. Perception of a space is often informed by perception of sounds experienced within that space. The positive perception we attribute to most nature sounds, even at low volumes, allows these sounds to mask distracting noises more effectively than traditional masking methods.[24]

Psychological ecosystem services. Defined in 2019 by Greg Bratman and colleagues as 'the positive mental health values of engaging with nature' indicated by natural features, exposure and proximity to nature, experiential characteristics and potential health impacts.[25] For projects with a landscape component, this can be incorporated into ecosystem service assessments.

Red List. A compendium of the 'worst in class materials prevalent in the building industry',[26] the Red List is not directly related to biophilic design. However, products that off-gas unnatural odours may diminish a biophilic experience, and products or components of a biophilic solution that contain red-listed chemicals may not be eligible for projects pursuing green building certification.

Skeuomorphism. The concept of making new objects that retain ornamental design cues that were inherent to the original real-world object. The pervasive 'email' icon on computers and smartphones, shaped like an envelope, is a skeuomorph. Biophilic examples would include a stool that is coloured and textured like a real tree stump, or a partition patterned like a bamboo grove. To be a successful biophilic intervention, skeuomorphs need to be either highly representational or truly exceptional so as to not disappoint the user upon discovering the true nature of the object.

Soft fascination. An environment that momentarily attracts our attention, sometimes referred to as 'soft fascination', feels effortless and allows other thoughts to occur simultaneously. Experiences of soft fascination are known to reduce stress and restore concentration and cognitive performance. Common examples include gazing at clouds, sunsets, crackling fires or water patterns.

Stochastic movement. A process, behaviour or occurrence with random or probabilistic components. A classic example is a random walk.

Thigmotaxis. A biological term characterising the motion or orientation of an organism (i.e. plant, insect, animal, human) either toward a solid object or in response to a touch stimulus, such as witnessed when a carnivorous plant retracts upon being touched or a mouse skirts the walls to get across a room. In the built environment, colloquial terms such as 'wall-hugging' or 'clear edge conditions' are used to describe this phenomenon, and which are emblematic of prospect-refuge theory — in wide open or steep spaces, humans are often positively thigmotactic, seeking an edge or cover for security or protection.

Topophilia. The affective bond between people and place and the resulting environmental perceptions and values;[27] also defined as a learnt response to place 'formed out of the familiar context of everyday living than in a genuine rootedness in the biology and topography of place'.[28]

K. 15 PATTERNS IN 7 LANGUAGES

DUTCH
15 BIOFILISCH ONTWERP PATRONEN: HET VERBETEREN VAN GEZONDHEID EN WELZIJN IN DE GEBOUWDE OMGEVING.

NATUUR IN DE RUIMTE	NATUURLIJKE ANALOGEN	NATUUR VAN DE RUIMTE
1. Visueel contact met de natuur 2. Non-visueel contact met de natuur 3. Non-ritmische zintuigelijke prikkels 4. Variatie in temperatuur en luchtstromen 5. Aanwezigheid van water 6. Dynamisch en diffuus licht 7. Contact met natuurlijke systemen	8. Biomorfe vormen en patronen 9. Contact met natuurlijke materialen 10. Complexiteit en orde	11. Vergezicht 12. Toevlucht 13. Mysterie 14. Risico / Gevaar 15. Verwondering / Ontzag

FILIPINO
15 MGA HULMA NG DISENYONG BIOPHILIC: PAGPAPABUTI NG KALUSUGAN AT KAPAKANAN NG MGA NAKATIRA GAWANG-TAONG KAPALIGIRAN.

KALIKASAN SA ESPASYO	NATURAL NA MGA ANALOGO	KALIKASAN NG ESPASYO
1. Nakikitang koneksyon sa kalikasan 2. Mga di nakikitang koneksyon sa kalikasan 3. Walang ritmong pamukaw sa pandama 4. Pagkakaiba-iba ng init at daloy ng hangin 5. Pagkakaroon ng tubig 6. Pagkakaiba iba at pagkakalat ng liwanag 7. Koneksyon sa mga natural na sistema	8. Hugis at dibuhong kalikasan 9. Materyal na koneksyon sa kalikasan 10. Masikot at maayos	11. Malawak na pagtingin / Panorama 12. Kanlungan / Shelter 13. Misteryo 14. Panganib 15. Kagilagilalas

FRENCH
15 MODÈLES DE CONCEPTION BIOPHILIQUE: STRATÉGIES DE CONCEPTION QUI PERMETTENT D'AMÉLIORER LA SANTÉ ET LE BIEN-ÊTRE DANS UN ENVIRONNEMENT CONSTRUIT.

NATURE DANS L'ESPACE	ANALOGIES NATURELLES	NATURE DE L'ESPACE
1. Lien visuel avec la nature 2. Lien non-visuel avec la nature 3. Stimulations sensorielles non-rythmiques 4. Variabilité thermique et renouvellement d'air 5. Présence de l'eau 6. Lumière dynamique et diffuse 7. Lien avec les systèmes naturels	8. Modèles et formes biomorphiques 9. Lien matériel avec la nature 10. Complexité et ordre	11. Perspective 12. Refuge 13. Mystère 14. Risque 15. Admiration / Impressionnant

GERMAN
15 MUSTER DES BIOPHILEN/BIOPHILIC DESIGNS.

NATUR IM RAUM	NATÜRLICHE ANALOGIEN	NATUR DES RAUMES
1. Visuelle verbindung mit der natur 2. Nicht visuelle verbindung mit der natur 3. Nicht-rhythmische sensorische stimuli 4. Thermal- und luftstromvariabilität 5. Präsenz von wasser 6. Dynamisches und diffuses licht 7. Verbindung mit natürlichen systemen	8. Biomorphe formen und muster 9. Materielle Verbindung mit der natur 10. Komplexität und ordnung	11. Aussicht 12. Zuflucht 13. Geheimnis 14. Risiko / Gefahr 15. Ehrfurcht (Ehrfurcht erregend)

ITALIAN
15 MODELLI BIOFILICI PER MIGLIORARE LA SALUTE E IL BENESSERE NELL'AMBIENTE COSTRUITO.

NATURA NELLO SPAZIO	SURROGATI NATURALI	NATURA DELLO SPAZIO
1. Connessione visiva con la natura 2. Connessione non visiva con la natura 3. Stimoli sensoriali non ritmici 4. Variabilità della temperatura e del flusso d'aria 5. Presenza dell'acqua 6. Luce diffusa e dinamica 7. Connessione con i sistemi naturali	8. Forme e motivi biomorfici 9. Connessione materiale con la natura 10. Ordine e complessità	11. Prospettiva 12. Rifugio 13. Mistero 14. Rischio e pericolo 15. Meraviglia

PORTUGUESE
15 PADRÕES DE DESIGN BIOFÍLICO: ESTRATÉGIAS DE DESIGN PARA MELHORAR A SAÚDE E O BEM-ESTAR NOS AMBIENTES CONSTRUÍDOS.

NATUREZA NO ESPAÇO	ANALOGIAS NATURAIS	NATUREZA DO ESPAÇO
1. Conexão Visual com a Natureza 2. Conexão Não-Visual com a Natureza 3. Estímulo Sensorial Não-Rítmico 4. Variação Térmica e de Fluxo de Ar 5. Presença de Água 6. Luz Dinâmica e Difusa 7. Conexão com os Sistemas Naturais	8. Formas e Padronagens Biomórficas 9. Conexão dos Materiais com a Natureza 10. Complexidade e Ordem	11. Panorama 12. Refúgio 13. Mistério 14. Risco / Perigo 15. Admiração

SPANISH
15 PATRONES DE DISEÑO BIOFÍLICO: ESTRATEGIAS DE DISEÑO PARA MEJORAR LA SALUD Y EL BIENESTAR DE LOS ENTORNOS CONSTRUIDOS.

NATURALEZA EN EL ESPACIO	ANALOGÍAS NATURALES	NATURALEZA DEL ESPACIO
1. Conexión visual con la naturaleza 2. Conexión no visual con la naturaleza 3. Estímulos sensoriales no rítmicos 4. Variabilidad térmica y de flujos de aire 5. Presencia de agua 6. Luz dinámica y difusa 7. Conexión con sistemas naturales	8. Formas y patrones biomórficos 9. Conexión de los materiales con la naturaleza 10. Complejidad y orden	11. Perspectiva 12. Refugio 13. Misterio 14. Riesgo / Peligro 15. Asombro

ACKNOWLEDGEMENTS

SPECIAL THANKS

To our RIBA editors, Elizabeth Webster and Clare Holloway, for giving us the freedom to write this book the way we had envisioned, and to Thomas Heatherwick for creating inspiring biophilic spaces and for graciously contributing his personal perspective in the foreword to this manuscript.

This work began at Rocky Mountain Institute as a result of investigating early examples of increased productivity in green buildings. Thanks to former RMI colleagues, Amory Lovins, Hunter Lovins, Joseph Romm, Benjamin Shepherd, Jenifer Seal–Cramer and Corey Griffin.

Special thanks to Edward O. Wilson, without whom this conversation would not be happening; and to Judith H. Heerwagen and the late Stephen R. Kellert for being the first to make the connection between biophilia and the built environment. Thank you also to Judi for first introducing Bill Browning to the concept of biophilia in 1995, to Chris Garvin for suggesting we write and publish 'The Economics of Biophilia' in 2012, and to Mary Davidge for supporting our research and development of the pattern language ever since.

The work has continued over the years with our team at Terrapin Bright Green. Thank you to Robert Fox, Richard Cook, Chris Garvin, Scott Andrews, Allison Bernett, Joseph Clancy, Georgina Davis, Lili Fisher, Sam Gochman, Alice Hartley, Namita Kallianpurkar, Travis Knop, Leslie Labruto, Rebecca Macies, Cory Nestor, Eleanor Sadik–Khan, Cas Smith, Chris Starkey, Rita Trombin, Dakota Walker, Jonce Walker and Siobhan Watson.

CONTRIBUTING THANKS

Thank you to the following individuals and firms who graciously contributed ideas, time and narratives to the making of this manuscript, and to the many others who have contributed photographs of their biophilic projects.

Joshua Aidlin, Aidlin Darling Design
Luca Baraldo, COOKFOX Architects DCP
Bethany Borel, COOKFOX Architects DCP
Leah Anne Bloom
Daan and Gijs Bruggink, ORGA Architect
Shao Yen Tan, CPG Corporation
Richard Cook, COOKFOX Architects DCP
Mary Davidge, Google
Jim Determan, Craig Gaulden Davis
Lorraine Francis, CADIZ Collaborative
Eric Gunther, Sosolimited
Richard Hassel, WOHA
Oliver Heath, Oliver Heath Design
Will Meyer, Meyer Davis
Peter O'Kennedy, Clodagh Design
Richard Piacentini, Phipps Conservatory and Botanical Gardens
Nadine Quirmbach, CannonDesign
Rebeca Ramos, formerly of Heatherwick Studio
C. Alan Short, Cambridge University
Kate Turpin, Google

COLLABORATIVE THANKS

To the many individuals who have been invaluable collaborators and staunch advocates or thought leaders in biophilic design, leading up to and during the creation of this manuscript.

Julia Kane Africa
Thomas Albright, The Salk Institute for Biological Studies
Sally Augustin, Design with Science
Charlie V. Balagtas, Partido State University
Timothy Beatley, University of Virginia
Evan Benway, The Sound Agency
Richard Berger, Clif Bar
Robert Berkebile, BNIM
Allison Bernett, Cornell University
Sonja Bochart, Shepley Bulfinch
Scott Booth, COOKFOX Architects DCP
Clark Brockman, SERA
Gail Brager, University of California Berkeley
Zafir Buraei, Pace University
Kevin Burke, Parabola
Elizabeth F. Calabrese, Calabrese Architects
Pamela Campbell, COOKFOX Architects DCP
Joseph O. Clancy, WSP
Nancy Clanton, Clanton & Associates, Inc.
Sir Cary Cooper, Robertson Cooper
Zachary Craun, COOKFOX Architects DCP
Chip DeGrace, Interface
Herbert Dreiseitl, Dreiseitl Consulting
Jacob Dunn, ZGF Architects
S. Richard Fedrizzi, International WELL Building Institute
Randy W. Fiser, American Society of Interior Designers
Chris W. Garvin, Google
David Gerson, Inscape
Raphael Dieter Gielgen, Vitra
Jared Gilbert, COOKFOX Architects DCP
Angelina Giro, formerly of Interface
Burt Gregory, Mithun
Robin Guenther, Perkins+Will
Elysa Hammond, Clif Bar
Elora Hardy, IBUKU

Clark Harris, Interface
Judith H. Heerwagen, U.S. General Services Administration
Lance Hosey, Gensler
Nicole Isle, Glumac
Erin Jende, Interface
Susan Kaplan, BuildingWrx
Cindy Kaufman, Interface
Stephen R. Kellert
David Kepron, Retail (r)Evolution, LLC
Claudio Lai, Art Aqua
Celine Larkin, Qatar Supreme Committee for Planning and Legacy
Vivian Loftness, Carnegie Mellon University
Nadav Malin, BuildingGreen
Kate Malmgren, formerly of Google
Malaysia Marshall, formerly of International Living Future Institute
Gayle Mault, Heatherwick Studio
Bruce McEvoy, Perkins+Will
Timothy McGee, formerly of International Living Future Institute
William McDonough, William McDonough + Partners
Carrie Meinberg Burke, Parabola
Tanya Mejia, RTKL
Heather Nelson, RTKL
Olin James Nettles
Peter Newman, Curtain University
Steven Nygren, Serenbe
David Oakey, David Oakey Designs
Georgy Olivieri
David Orr, Oberlin College
Susan Painter, AC Martin
Steven Peck, Green Roofs for Healthy Cities
Kari Pei, Interface
Liana Penabad–Camacho, Hispanoamericana University and
    National University of Costa Rica
Matt Piccone, SERA Architects
Marcela I. Pinilla
Kate Randolph, Google
Anthony Ravitz, Google
Mark Rusitzky, COOKFOX Architects DCP
Gene Sandoval, ZGF Architects
S. Bry Sarté, Sherwood Design Engineers

Roger Schickedantz, William McDonough + Partners
Jenifer Seal–Cramer
Stefano Serafini, International Society of Biourbanism
Chen Shalita, Alfa Projects
Benjamin Shepherd, Atelier Ten
Jana Soderlund, Biophilic Solutions
Ally Stoneham, International Living Future Institute
Amanda Sturgeon, formerly of International Living Future Institute
Raphael Sperry, ARUP
Ann Sussman, architect, author and researcher
Susan Szenasy, Metropolis
Phillip Tabb, Phill Tabb Studio
Rives Taylor, Gensler
Stella Tarnay, Capital Nature – Biophilic DC
Susie Teal, COOKFOX Architects DCP
Heidi Theunissen, ODA Architecture
Joe Van Belleghem, Google
Helena van Vliet, Helena van Vliet Architect
James Waddell, Cognitive Corp.
Sue Weidemann, Center for Inclusive Design and
    Environmental Access
Richard E. Wener, New York University
Florence Williams
Alex Wilson, BuildingGreen
Kendall Wilson, Perkins+Will
Emily Winer, International WELL Building Institute
Wong Mun Summ, WOHA
Joe Zazzera, Plant Solutions Inc.

INDUSTRY LEADERSHIP THANKS
To the organisations who have collaboratively led the way in making biophilic design accessible to the broader public.

American Society of Interior Designers
ARP–Astrance
ArtAqua
Biophilic Cities
BRE Group
Clif Bar
Clodagh Design
COOKFOX Architects DCP
Delos
Google
Heatherwick Studio
Interface
International Living Future Institute
International WELL Building Institute
Lake|Flato
Oliver Heath Design
Metropolis Magazine
Perkins+Will
Phipps Conservatory and Botanical Gardens
SERA Architects
Snøhetta
Terrapin Bright Green WOHA
The Biophilic Institute
USGBC
ZGF Architects

ACADEMIC THANKS

To the many academics who continue to build the science base for biophilic design. We are grateful for your dedication as we relentlessly and shamelessly promote your research and publications.

Belal Abboushi, Pacific Northwest National Laboratory
C. Alan Short, University of Cambridge
Joseph G. Alan, Harvard University
Jo Barton, University of Essex
Irving Biederman, University of Southern California
Gail Brager, University of California Berkeley
Gregory N. Bratman, University of Washington
John D. Spengler, Center for Health and the Global Environment, Harvard University
Payam Dadvand, Center for Research in Environmental Epidemiology, IS Global
Zakaria Djebbara, Aaberg University
Ihab M.K. Elzeyadi, University of Oregon
Howard Frumkin, University of Washington
Caroline M. Hägerhäll, Swedish University of Agricultural Sciences
Terry Hartig, Uppsala University
Lisa Heschong, Heschong Mahone Group
Grant Hildebrand, University of Washington
Yannick Joye, University of Groningen
Peter H. Kahn, Jr., University of Washington
Rachel Kaplan, University of Michigan
Stephen Kaplan, University of Michigan
Nirmal Tulsidas Kishnani, National University of Singapore
Kalevi M. Korpela, University of Tampere
Andreas Liebl, Fraunhofer Institute for Building Physics, IBP
Alan Laird Lewis, The New England College of Optometry
Qing Li, Nippon Medical School
Michael Mehaffy, University of Oregon
Yoshifumi Miyazaki, Chiba National University
Gordon Orians, University of Washington
Bum-Jin Park, Chungnam National University
Jules Pretty, University of Essex
Nikos A. Salingaros, University of Texas at San Antonio
Kamal Sen, Boston University

Mardelle Shepley, Cornell University
Richard Taylor, University of Oregon
Yuko Tsunetsugu, Forestry and Forest Products Research Institute
Liisa Tyrväinen, Finnish Forest Research Institute
Rohit Verma, Cornell University
Edward A. Vessel, Max–Planck–Institut für Empirische Ästhetik
Roger S. Ulrich, Chalmers University of Technology
Jie Yin, Harvard University

INSPIRATIONAL THANKS

To the individuals whose vision and philosophy have inspired our work.

Christopher Alexander
Jay Appleton
Janine Benyus
Rachel Carson
Jacques Cousteau
R. Buckminster Fuller
Stephen R. Kellert
Richard Louv
Amory Lovins
John Muir
Frederick Law Olmsted
Edward O. Wilson
Frank Lloyd Wright

REFERENCES

INTRODUCTION

1   Catherine O. Ryan and William D. Browning, 'Biophilic Design' in *Encyclopedia of Sustainability Science and Technology*, ed. R.A. Meyers, 2017, pp. 1–2, https://doi.org/10.1007/978-1-4939-2493-6_1034-1

2   Erich Fromm, *The Heart of Man: Its Genius for Good and Evil*, Harper & Row, 1964.

3   Edward O. Wilson, *Biophilia: The Human Bond with Other Species*, Cambridge, Harvard University Press, 1984.

4   Jay Appleton, *Experience of Landscape*, New York, John Wiley & Sons, 1975.

5   Gordon Orians and Judith Heerwagen, 'Evolved Responses to Landscapes' in *The Adapted Mind: Evolutionary Psychology and the Generation of Culture*, eds J. Barkow, L. Cosmides and J. Tooby, Oxford and New York, Oxford University Press, 1992.

6   Vitaly Komar and Alex Melamid, 'The Most Wanted Paintings', *Artist Web Projects*, Dia Art Foundation, launch date 5 September 1995. https://www.diaart.org/program/exhibitions-projects/komar-melamid-the-most-wanted-paintings-web-project/komar-melamid-the-most-wanted-paintings-web-project/index.html

7   Judith Heerwagen and Gordon Orians, 'Humans, Habitats and Aesthetics' in *The Biophilia Hypothesis*, eds Stephen Kellert and E.O. Wilson, Washington, DC, Island Press, 1993, pp. 138–172.

8   Jenifer S. Cramer and William D. Browning, 'Transforming Building Practices Through Biophilic Design' in *Biophilic Design*, eds Stephen F. Kellert, Judith H. Heerwagen and Martin L. Mador, Hoboken, Wiley, 2008, pp. 335–346.

9   William D. Browning, Catherine O. Ryan and Joseph O. Clancy, *14 Patterns of Biophilic Design: Improving Health & Well-Being in the Built Environment*, New York, Terrapin Bright Green, 2014. https://www.terrapinbrightgreen.com/reports/14-patterns/

10 ibid., p. 39.

11 ibid.

12 Carlo Ratti, Antoine Picone, Alex Haw and Matthew Claudel, 'The power of networks: Beyond Critical Regionalism', *The Architectural Review*, https://www.architectural-review.com/essays/the-power-of-networks-beyond-critical-regionalism/8651014.article, 23 July, 2013, (accessed on 1 March 2020).

CHAPTER 1

1   Edward O. Wilson, 'Biophilia and the Conservation Ethic' in *The Biophilia Hypothesis*, eds Stephen R. Kellert and Edward O. Wilson, Washington DC, Island Press, 1993, p. 31.

2   Roger Ulrich, 'View Through a Window May Influence Recovery from Surgery', *Science*, Vol. 27, 1984, pp. 420–421.

3   Roger Ulrich & Outi Lunden, 'Effects of Nature and Abstract Pictures on Patients Recovering from Open-Heart Surgery', *Paper presented at the International Congress of Behavioral Medicine*, Uppsala, Sweden, 1990, pp. 27–30.

4   Batya Friedman, Nathan G. Freier, Peter H. Kahn Jr, Peyina Lin & Robin Sodeman, 'Office window of the future? Field-based analyses of a new use of a large display', *International Journal of Human-Computer Studies*, Vol. 66, 2008, pp. 452–465.

5   Peter H. Kahn, Batya Friedman, Brian Gill, Jennifer Hagman, Rachel L. Severson, Nathan G. Freier, Erika N. Feldman, Sybil Carrere & Anna Stolyar, 'A plasma display window? The shifting baseline problem in a technologically mediated natural world', *Journal of Environmental Psychology*, Vol. 28, 2008, pp. 192–199.

6   Irving Biederman & Edward Vessel, 'Perceptual pleasure and the brain', *American Scientist*, Vol. 94, 2006, pp. 249–255.

7   Ann Sussman & Justin Hollander, *Cognitive Architecture: Designing How We Respond to The Built Environment*, Routledge, Abingdon, 2015.

8   Michael Beauchamp, Kathryn Lee, James Haxby & Alex Martin, 'fMRI Responses to Video and Point-Light Displays of Moving Humans and Manipulable Objects', *Journal of Cognitive Neuroscience*, Vol. 15, issue 7, Cambridge, Massachusetts Institute of Technology, 2003, pp. 991–1001.

9   Michael D. Hunter, Simon B. Eickhoff, Robert J. Pheasant, M.J. Douglas, Greg R. Watts, Tom F.D. Farrow, D. Hyland, Jian Kang, I.D. Wilkinson, K.V. Horoshenkov & Peter W.R. Woodruff, 'The state of tranquillity: Subjective perception is shaped by contextual modulation of auditory connectivity', *Neuroimage*, Vol. 53, 2010, pp. 611–618.

10 Yuko Tsunetsugu, Ji-Young Lee, Bum-Jin Park, Liisa Tyrväinen, Takahide Kagawa & Yoshifumi Miyazaki, 'Physiological and psychological effects of viewing urban forest Tsunetsugu landscapes assessed by multiple measurements', *Landscape and Urban Planning*, Vol. 113, 2013, pp. 90–93.

11 Bum-Jin Park, Yuko Tsunetsugu, Tanami Kasetani, Takeshi Morikawa, Takahide Kagawa & Yoshifumi Miyazaki, 'Physiological Effects of Forest Recreation in a Young Conifer Forest in Hinokage Town, Japan', *Silva Fennica*, Vol. 43, issue 2, 2009, pp. 291–301.

12 Qing Li, 'Effect of forest bathing trips on human immune function', *Environmental Health and Preventive Medicine*, Vol. 15, 2010, pp. 9–17. https://doi.org/10.1007/s12199-008-0068-3

13 Hiroki Harada, Hideki Kashiwadani, Yuichi Kanmura & Tomayuki Kuwaki, 'Linalool Odor-Induced Anxiolytic Effects in Mice', *Frontiers in Behavioral Neuroscience*, 23 October 2018. https://doi.org/10.3389/fnbeh.2018.00241

14 Frederick Law Olmsted, *Yosemite and the Mariposa Grove: A Preliminary Report 1865, (Introduction)*, Report to the US Congress, Washington DC, 1865, Yosemite Association, https://www.yosemite.ca.us/library/olmsted/, 1993, (accessed on 1 May 2020).

15 Rachel Kaplan & Stephen Kaplan, *The Experience of Nature: A Psychological Perspective*, Cambridge University Press, Cambridge, 1989.

16 Stephen Kaplan, 'The restorative benefits of nature: Toward an integrative framework', *Journal of Environmental Psychology*, Vol. 15, issue 3, 1995, pp. 169–182.

17   Kate E. Lee, Kathryn J.H. Williams, Leisa D. Sargent, Nicholas S.G. Williams & Katherine A. Johnson, '40–second green roof views sustain attention: The role of micro–breaks in attention restoration', *Journal of Environmental Psychology*, Vol. 42, 2015, pp. 182–189.

18   Payam Dadvand, Mark J. Nieuwenhuijsen, Mikel Esnaola, Joan Forns, Xavier Basagaña, Mar Alvarez–Pedrerol, Ioar Rivas, Monica López–Vicentea, Montserrat De Castro Pascual, Jason Su, Michael Jerrett, Xavier Querol & Jordi Sunyer, 'Green spaces and cognitive development in primary schoolchildren', *Proceedings of the National Academy of Sciences of the United States of America,* Vol. 112, issue 26, 2015, pp. 7937–7942.

19   Jie Yin, Shihao Zhu, Piers MacNaughton, Joseph G. Allen & John D. Spengler, 'Physiological and cognitive performance of exposure to biophilic indoor environment', *Building and Environment*, Vol. 132, 2018, pp. 255–262.

20   Ihab Elzeyadi, 'Daylighting–Bias and Biophilia: Quantifying the Impacts of Daylighting on Occupants Health', *Thought and Leadership in Green Buildings Research. Greenbuild 2011 Proceedings*, USGBC Press, Washington, DC, 2011. https://www.usgbc.org/sites/default/files/OR10_Daylighting%20Bias%20and%20Biophilia.pdf

21   For calculation explanation see: Dakota Walker, Catherine O. Ryan, William J. Browning & Rebecca Macies, 'The Economics of Biophilia: Why designing with nature in mind makes financial sense', Terrapin Bright Green, New York, NY, Second edition, 2020.

22   BOMA International, 'BOMA International's Office and Industrial Benchmarking Reports Released', BOMA International & Kingsley Associates, https://www.boma.org/BOMA/Research-Resources/3-BOMA–Spaces/Newsroom/PR91818.aspx, 2018, (accessed on 10 December 2019).

23   BOMA International, 'BOMA 2016 Office Experience Exchange Report', cited in Facility Executive, 'BOMA 2016 Experience Exchange Reports Released', https://facilityexecutive.com/2016/07/boma-2016-experience-exchange-reports/, 2016, (accessed on 10 December 2019).

24   Bureau of Labor Statistics, 'Employer Costs for Employee Compensation: Table 4. Employer Costs for Employee Compensation for private industry workers by occupational and industry group', US Department of Labor, Washington, D.C., https://www.bls.gov/news.release/archives/ecec_12182019.htm, 2019, (accessed on 5 May 2020).

25   Bureau of Labor Statistics, 'Labor Force Statistics from the Current Population Survey: Household data annual averages: Table 47. Absences from work of employed full-time wage and salary workers by occupation and industry', US Department of Labor. Washington, D.C., https://www.bls.gov/cps/cpsaat47.htm, 2020, (accessed on 5 May 2020).

26   Cushman & Wakefield, 'Space Matters: Key office trends and metrics for US occupiers', Cushman & Wakefield – Research & Insights, http://www.cushmanwakefield.us/en/research-and-insight/2018/space-matters, 2018, (accessed 12 December 2019).

27   Lee et al., ibid.

28   Lisa Heschong, Heschong Mahone Group, 'Windows and Offices: A Study of Office Worker Performance and the Indoor Environment', California Energy Commission: Pacific Gas and Electric Company, http://h-m-g.com/downloads/Daylighting/A-9_Windows_Offices_2.6.10.pdf, 2003, (accessed 23 March 2020).

29   Vivian Loftness, 'Sustainable Design for Health & Productivity', *Carnegie Mellon University, Center for Building Performance & Diagnostics*, Pittsburgh, PA, 2008.

30   Joseph J. Romm & William D. Browning, 'Greening the Building and the Bottom Line: Increasing Productivity Through Energy-Efficient Design', Rocky Mountain Institute, https://rmi.org/insight/greening-the-building-and-the-bottom-line/, 1994, (accessed 23 March 2020).

31   Kathleen L. Wolf, 'Trees in the small city retail business district: comparing resident and visitor perceptions', *Journal of Forestry,* Vol. 103, 2005, pp. 390–395.

32   Sonja Windhager, Klaus Atzwanger, Fred L. Brookstein & Katrin Schaefer, 'Fish in a mall aquarium – An ethological investigation of biophilia', *Landscape and Urban Planning,* Vol. 99, 2011, pp. 23–30.

33   Earl D. Benson, Julia L. Hansen, Arthur L. Jr. Schwartz & Greg T. Smersh, 'Pricing Residential Amenities: The Value of a View', *The Journal of Real Estate Finance and Economics*, Vol. 16, issue 1, 1998, pp. 55–73.

34   William D. Browning, Catherine O. Ryan, Rebecca Macies, Lilli Fisher & Lorraine Francis, 'Human Spaces 2.0: Biophilic Design in Hospitality, *Interface,* http://interfaceinc.scene7.com/is/content/InterfaceInc/Interface/Americas/WebsiteContentAssets/Documents/Reports/Hosp-Human%20Spaces/wc_am-interfacehospitalityhumanspaces8252017.pdf, 2017, (accessed 23 March 2020).

35   Ulrich & Lunden, ibid.

36   US Department of Health and Human Services, *National hospital discharge survey: 2010 tables, number of all-listed procedures for discharges from short-stay hospitals, by procedure category and age: United States*, National Center for Health Statistics, 2010.

37   Lisa Mirel & Kelly Carper, *Expenses for Hospital Inpatient Stays 2010*, Statistical Brief #401, Rockville, MD, Agency for Healthcare Research and Quality, 2013. http://www.meps.ahrq.gov/mepsweb/data_files/publications/st401/stat401.pdf, (accessed 23 March 2020).

38   Terrapin Bright Green, 'The Economics of Biophilia: Healthcare', PRISM, https://prismpub.com/the-economics-of-biophilia-healthcare/, 2018, (accessed 11 May 2020).

39   Claire C. Marcus & Marni Barnes, *Gardens in Healthcare Facilities: Uses, Therapeutic Benefits, and Design Recommendations*, University of California Berkeley, The Center for Health Design, 1995.

40   Michael H. Nicklas & Gary B. Bailey, 'Student Performance in Daylit Schools', *Innovative Design*, Raleigh, North Carolina, 1996.

41   Lisa Heschong, Heschong Mahone Group, 'Daylighting in Schools: An Investigation into the Relationship Between Daylighting and Human Performance', *Pacific Gas and Electric Company*, 1999 https://www.pge.com/includes/docs/pdfs/shared/edusafety/training/pec/daylight/SchoolsCondensed820.pdf, 1999, (accessed 23 March 2020).

42   Dongying Li & William C. Sullivan, 'Impact of views to school landscapes on recovery from stress and mental fatigue', *Landscape and Urban Planning*, Vol. 148, 2016, pp. 149–158.

CHAPTER 2

1   Stephen R. Kellert and Elizabeth F. Calabrese, 'The Practice of Biophilic Design', http://www.biophilic-design.com, 2015, pp. 6–7 (accessed 23 March 2020).

2   The Stephen R. Kellert Biophilic Design Award, International Living Future Institute, https://living-future.org/biophilic-design-award/

CHAPTER 4

1   Grant Hildebrand, *The Wright Space: Pattern and Meaning in Frank Lloyd Wright's Houses*, University of Washington Press, Seattle, 1991.

2   Stephen R. Kellert, *Kinship to Mastery*, Island Press, Washington DC, 1997, pp. 166–167.

3   Study demonstrated a margin of 20% between girls with and without a view to green space. Andrea Faber Taylor, Frances E. Kuo & William C. Sullivan, 'Views of Nature and Self-Discipline: Evidence from Inner City Children', *Journal of Environmental Psychology, 22*(1–2), 2001, pp. 49–63.

4   Helena van Vliet, Biophilic Design — a definition of Refuge and Prospect, Helena van Vliet Architecture LLC, https://www.helenavanvliet.com/#biophilic–design, (accessed 17 October 2019).

5   *Private family residence of Kelly Hoppen MBE*, 2015, retrieved 25 October 2019, from Kelly Hoppen MBE.

6   Luca Baraldo, '1 Columbus Place Qs' [email to C.O. Ryan], 4 November 2019 (accessed 8 November 2019).

CHAPTER 5

1   Tina Bruce, ed., *Early Childhood Practice: Froebel Today*, SAGE Publications Ltd, Thousand Oaks, CA, 2012, doi: http://dx.doi.org/10.4135/9781446251287

2   Michael H. Nicklas & Gary B. Bailey, 'Student Performance in Daylit Schools', *Innovative Design – Reports*, http://www.innovativedesign.net/wp-content/uploads/2019/05/Analysis-of-Student-Performance–in-Daylit-Schools.pdf, 1996, (accessed 1 November 2019).

3   Lisa Heschong, Heschong Mahone Group, 'Daylighting in Schools: An Investigation into the Relationship Between Daylighting and Human Performance, *Pacific Gas and Electric Company*, https://www.pge.com/includes/docs/pdfs/shared/edusafety/training/pec/daylight/SchoolsCondensed820.pdf, 1999, (accessed 1 November 2019).

4   Dongying Li & William C. Sullivan, 'Impact of views to school landscapes on recovery from stress and mental fatigue', *Landscape and Urban Planning,* Vol. 148, 2016, pp. 149–158.

5   Jie Yin, Shihao Zhu, Piers MacNaughton, Joseph G. Allen & John D. Spengler, 'Physiological and cognitive performance of exposure to biophilic indoor environment', *Building and Environment* Vol. 132, 2018, pp. 255–262.

6   Rodney H. Matsuoka, 'Student performance and high school landscapes: Examining the links', *Landscape and Urban Planning,* Vol. 97, issue 4, 2010, pp. 273–282.

7   Payam Dadvand, Mark J. Nieuwenhuijsen, Mikel Esnaola, Joan Forns, Xavier Basagaña, Mar Alvarez-Pedrerol, Ioar Rivas, Mónica López-Vicentea, Montserrat De Castro Pascual, Jason Su, Michael Jerrett, Xavier Querol & Jordi Sunyer, 'Green spaces and cognitive development in primary schoolchildren', *Proceedings of the National Academy of Sciences of the United States of America,* Vol. 112, issue 26, 2015, pp. 7937–7942.

8   Heschong, ibid.

9   Nicklas and Bailey, ibid.

10 Gregory Kats, 'Greening America's Schools – Cost and Benefits', *Capital E – Report*, The US Green Building Council, https://www.usgbc.org/resources/greening-america039s-schools-costs-and-benefits, 2006.

11 Ming Kuo, Matthew H.E.M. Browning & Milbert L. Penner, 'Do lessons in nature boost subsequent classroom engagement? Refueling students in flighting', *Frontiers in Psychology,* Vol. 8, 2018, p. 2253.

12 Li & Sullivan, ibid.

13 Nancy M. Wells and Gary W. Evans, 'Nearby Nature: A Buffer of Life Stress Among Rural Children', *Environment and Behavior,* Vol. 35, issue 3, 2003, pp. 311–330.

14 David Orr, *Earth in Mind*, Island Press, Washington DC, 1994, p. 113.

15 James Determan, Thomas Albright, William Browning, Mary Anne Akers, Paul Archibald, Catherine Martin-Dunlop & Valerie Caruolo, 'The Impact of Biophilic Design on Student Success', *American Institute of Architects Building Research Information Knowledgebase*, 2019.

16 Hadeer Abd-El-Razak Barakat, Ali Bakr & Zeyad El-Syad, 'Nature as a healer for autistic children', *Alexandria Engineering Journal*, Vol. 58, issue 1, 2019, pp. 353–366.

17 Ihab M. K. Elzeyadi, 'Quantifying the Impacts of Green Schools on People and Planet', in *Proceedings of the 2012 Greenbuild Conference*, San Francisco, 2012, pp. 48–60.

18 C. Alan Short, *The Recovery of Natural Environments in Architecture*, Earthscan, Routledge, Oxon, 2017, pp. 75–78.

CHAPTER 6

1   Judith H. Heerwagen, 'Design, Productivity and Well Being: What are the Links?' Presented at AIA Conference on Highly Effective Facilities, Cincinnati, OH, 1998.

2   Yannick Joye, Kim Willem, Malaika Brengman, & Kathleen Wolf, 'The effects of urban retail greenery on consumer experience', *Urban Forestry & Urban Gardening*, Vol. 9, 2010, pp. 57–64.

3   KPMG, Global Retail Trends 2018, KPMG Global Consumer & Retail Team, 2018, https://home.kpmg/xx/en/home/insights/2018/03/2018-retail-trends.html

4   Sonja Windhager, Klaus Atzwanger, Fred L. Bookstein & Katrin Schaefer, 'Fish in a mall aquarium – An ethological investigation of biophilia', *Landscape and Urban Planning*, Vol. 99, 2011, pp. 21–30.

5   Richard L. Kent, 'The Role of Mystery in Preferences for Shopping Malls', *Landscape Journal*, Vol. 8, 1989, pp. 28–35.

6   Joseph J. Romm & William D. Browning, 'Greening the Building and the Bottom Line', Rocky Mountain Institute, Snowmass, Colorado, 1994.

7   Lisa Heschong, Heschong Mahone Group, 'Daylight and Retail Sales', California Energy Commission: Pacific Gas and Electric Company, Fair Oaks, California, 2003.

8   Kathleen L. Wolf, 'Trees in the small city retail business district: comparing resident and visitor perceptions', *Journal of Forestry*, Vol. 103, 2005, pp. 390–395.

CHAPTER 7

1   Joseph J. Romm & William D. Browning, 'Greening the Building and the Bottom Line: Increasing Productivity Through Energy-Efficient Design', Rocky Mountain Institute, https://rmi.org/insight/greening-the-building-and-the-bottom-line/, 1994, (accessed 10 September 2019).

2   Romm & Browning, ibid.

3   Jolanda Maas, 'Take a hike! How attention restoration theory shows that nature sharpens the mind', *Ode for Intelligent Optimists*, Vol. 8, issue 4, 2011.

4   Lisa Heschong, Heschong Mahone Group, 'Windows and Offices: A Study of Office Worker Performance and the Indoor Environment', California Energy Commission: Pacific Gas and Electric Company, http://h-m-g.com/downloads/Daylighting/A-9_Windows_Offices_2.6.10.pdf, 2003, (accessed 2 July 2019).

5   Vivian Loftness, 'Sustainable Design for Health & Productivity', Center for Building Performance & Diagnostics, 2008.

6   Ihab M. Elzeyadi, 'Daylighting–Bias and Biophilia: Quantifying the Impacts of Daylight on Occupants Health', in *Greenbuild 2011 Proceedings, Thought and Leadership in Green Buildings Research*, Washington, DC, USGBC Press, 2011.

7   Mariana G. Figueiro, Mark S. Rea, Anne C. Rea & Richard G. Stevens, 'Daylighting and productivity – A field study', in *Proceedings of the 2002 ACEEE Summer Study on Energy Efficiency in Buildings, Volume 8: Human and Social Dimensions of Energy Use: Understanding Markets and Demand*. Rensselaer Polytechnic Institute, 2002.

8   Mohamed Boubekri, Ivy N. Cheung, Kathryn J. Reid, Chia-Hui Wang & Phyllis C. Zee, 'Impact of Windows and Daylight Exposure on Overall Health and Sleep Quality of Office Workers: A Case-Control Pilot Study', *Journal of Clinical Sleep Medicine*, Vol. 10, issue 6, 2014, pp. 603–611.

9   Valtteri Hongisto, Annu Haapakangas & Miia Haka, 'Task performance and speech intelligibility – a model to promote noise control actions in open offices, *9th International Congress on Noise as a Public Health Problem (ICBEN)*, 2008.

10 Annu Haapakangas, E. Kankkunen, Valtteri Hongisto, Petra Virjonen & Esko Keskinen, 'Effects of Five Speech Masking Sounds on Performance and Acoustic Satisfaction. Implications for Open-Plan Offices', *ACTA Acustica United with Acustica*, Vol. 97, 2011, pp. 641–655.

11 Simon P. Banbury & Dianne C. Berry, 'Office noise and employee concentration: identifying causes of disruption and potential improvements', *Ergonomics*, Vol. 48, issue 1, 2005, pp. 25–37. doi: 10.1080/00140130412331311390

12 Simon P. Banbury & Dianne Berry, 'Disruption of office-related tasks by speech and office noise', *British Journal of Psychology*, Vol. 89, 1998, pp. 499–517. https://doi.org/10.1111/j.2044-8295.1998.tb02699.x

13 Alan G. DeLoach, Jeff P. Carter & Jonas Braasch, 'Tuning the cognitive environment: Sound masking with "natural" sounds in open-plan offices', *Journal of the Acoustical Society of America*, Vol. 137, issue 4, 2015, p. 2291.

14 Robert J. Pheasant, Mark N. Fisher, Greg R. Watts, David J. Whitaker & Kirill V. Horoshenkov, 'The importance of auditory-visual interaction in the construction of 'tranquil space', *Journal of Environmental Psychology*, Vol. 30, 2010, pp. 501–509.

15 American Society of Interior Designers, 'Impact of Design Series, Volume 1: ASID HQ Office', *American Society of Interior Designers Research*, https://www.asid.org/impact-of-design/asid, 2018, (accessed 8 September 2019).

CHAPTER 8

1   For greater depth on biophilic design patterns and trends in hospitality, see William D. Browning, Catherine O. Ryan, Rebecca Macies, Lilli Fisher & Lorraine Francis, 'Human Spaces 2.0: Biophilic Design in Hospitality, *Interface*, http://interfaceinc.scene7.com/is/content/InterfaceInc/Interface/Americas/WebsiteContentAssets/Documents/Reports/Hosp-Human%20Spaces/wc_am-interfacehospitalityhumanspaces8252017.pdf, 2017, (accessed 10 July 2019).

2   Lauren Powell, 'Rethinking Luxury Hotel Design to Connect Guests with Nature', *Skift*, https://skift.com/2019/10/15/rethinking-luxury-hotel-design-to-connect-guests-with-nature/, 2019, (accessed 15 October 2019).

3   Septy Diantari, 'TRi Restaurant', IBUKU, https://ibuku.com/tri-restaurant/, 2015, (accessed 16 October 2019).

4   Putri Wiwohoi, 'TRi Restaurant', IBUKU, https://ibuku.com/tri-restaurant/, 2015, (accessed 16 October 2019).

CHAPTER 9

1   Esther Sternberg, *Healing Environments, The Science of Place and Well-being*, Harvard University Press, Cambridge, 2009.

2   Roger S. Ulrich, Craig Zimring, Xiaobo Quan & Anjali Joseph, 'The environment's impact on stress' in *Improving Healthcare with Better Building Design*, ed. S. Marberry, Health Administration Press, Chicago, 2006, pp. 37–61.

3   Bernadette M. Melnyk, Liana Orsolini, Alai Tan, Cynthia Arslanian-Engorer, Gail D'eramo Melkus, Jacqueline Dunbar-Jacob, Virginia H. Rice, Angelica Millan, Sandra B. Dunbar, Lynne T. Braun, JoEllen Wilbur, Deborah A. Chyun, Kate Gawlik & Lisa M. Lewis, 'A National Study Links Nurses' Physical and Mental Health to Medical Errors and Perceived Worksite Wellness', *Journal of Occupational and Environmental Medicine*, Vol. 60, issue 2, 2018, pp. 126–131.

4   Roger S. Ulrich, 'View through a window may influence recovery from surgery', *Science*, Vol. 224, 1984, pp. 420–421.

5   Blair L. Sadler, Jennifer R. DuBose, Eileen B. Malone & Carl M. Zimring, 'Healthcare Leadership: The Business Case for Building Better Hospitals through Evidence Based Design', *Health Environments Research & Design Journal*, Vol. 1, issue 3, 2008, pp. 22–39.

6   Kathleen M. Beauchemin & Peter Hays, 'Sunny hospital rooms expedite recovery', *Journal of Affective Disorders*, Vol. 40, 1996, pp. 49–51.

7   Joon-Ho Choi, Liliana O. Beltran & Hway-Suh Kim, 'Impacts of indoor daylight environments on patient average length of stay (ALOS) in a healthcare facility', *Building and Environment*, Vol. 50, 2012, pp. 65–75.

8   Francesco Benedetti, Cristina Colombo, Barbara Barbini, Euridice Campori & Enrico Smeraldi, 'Morning sunlight reduces length of hospitalization in bipolar depression', *Journal of Affective Disorders*, Vol. 62, 2001, pp. 221–223.

9   Roger S. Ulrich, 'View through a window may influence recovery from surgery', *Science*, Vol. 224, 1984, pp. 420–421.

10 Jeffrey M. Walch, Bruce S. Rabin, Richard Day, Jessica N. Williams, Krissy Choi & James D. Kang, 'The Effect of Sunlight on Postoperative Analgesic Medication Use', *Psychosomatic Medicine*, Vol. 67, 2005, pp. 156–163.

11   Blair L. Sadler, Jennifer R. DuBose, Eileen B. Malone & Carl M. Zimring, 'Healthcare Leadership: The Business Case for Building Better Hospitals through Evidence Based Design', *Health Environments Research & Design Journal*, Vol. 1, issue 3, 2008, pp. 22–39.

12   Clare C. Marcus & Marni Barnes, 'Gardens in Healthcare Facilities: Uses, Therapeutic Benefits, and Design Recommendation' University of California at Berkeley. The Center for Health Design–Knowledge Repository, https://www.healthdesign.org/sites/default/files/Gardens%20in%20HC%20Facility%20Visits.pdf,1995, (accessed 5 November 2019).

13   Cannon Design, 'Ushering in a New Era in Specialty Inpatient Care', *Cannon Design–Work*, https://www.cannondesign.com/our–work/work/uc–san–diego–jacobs–medical–center/, (accessed 4 April 2019).

14   Email communication from Daan Bruggink, ORGA Architects, 23 October 2019.

15   Lena From & Stefan Lundig, *Architecture as Medicine – the Importance of Architecture for Treatment Outcomes in Psychiatry,* ARQ — the Architecture Research Foundation, Uppsala, Sweden, 2010.

CHAPTER 10

1   See H. M. Parsons, 'What Happened at Hawthorne?', *Science,* Vol. 183, No. 4128, pp. 922–932, 1974, for survey of original publications, news and interviews related to the original studies conducted in 1924–1932.

2   Michiel A.J. Kompier, 'The "Hawthorne effect" is a myth, but what keeps the story going?' *Scandinavian Journal of Work, Environment & Health,* Vol. 32(5), 2006, pp. 402–412.

3   H. M. Parsons, 'What Happened at Hawthorne?', *Science,* Vol. 183, No. 4128, pp. 922–932, 1974 (accessed on 21 May 2010).

4   Kompier, ibid.

5   Joseph J. Romm & William D. Browning, 'Greening the Building and the Bottom Line: Increasing Productivity Through Energy-Efficient Design', Rocky Mountain Institute, https://rmi.org/insight/greening-the-building-and-the-bottom-line/, 1994, (accessed 10 September 2019).

6   Judith H. Heerwagen, James Wise, David Lantrip & Michael Ivanovich, 'A Tale of Two Buildings: Biophilia and the Benefits of Green Design', *Paper presented at the U.S. Green Buildings Council Conference*, 17–20 November, US Green Building Council, San Diego, 1996.

7   Judith H. Heerwagen & Betty Hase, 'Building Biophilia: Connecting People to Nature in Building Design', US Green Building Council, https://www.usgbc.org/drupal/legacy/usgbc/docs/Archive/External/Docs8543.pdf, 2001, (accessed 9 July 2019).

8   For example, Peter H. Kahn, Jr, Batya Friedman, Brian Gill, Jennifer Hagman, Rachel L. Severson, Nathan G. Freier, Erika N. Feldman, Sybil Carrere & Anna Stolyar, 'A Plasma Display Window? The Shifting Baseline Problem in a Technology Mediated Natural World', *Journal of Environmental Psychology, Vol. 28(1), 2008,* pp. 192–199.

CHAPTER 11

1   Ray Oldenburg, *The Great Good Place*, Paragon House, New York, 1989.

2   The Center for Active Design, *Assembly: Civic Design Guidelines*, New York, 2018, p. 46.

3   Paul K. Piff, Pia Dietze, Matthew Feinberg, Daniel M. Stancato & Dacher Keltner, 'Awe, the small self, and prosocial behavior', *Journal of Personality and Social Psychology*, Vol. 108, issue 6, 2015, pp. 883–899. http://dx.doi.org/10.1037/pspi0000018

4   Personal communication with Sarah Meilleur, Director, Service Delivery, Calgary Public Library, 6 November 2019.

5   ibid.

CHAPTER 12

1   WIRRAL, 'Birkenhead Park: The world's first', *Wirral*, https://www.wirral.gov.uk/sites/default/files/all/Leisure%20parks%20and%20events/parks%20and%20open%20spaces/Birkenhead%20Park%20Management%20Plan%202018%20-%202022.pdf, (accessed 7 November 2019).

2   Frederick Law Olmsted, *Walks and Talks of an American Farmer in England*, George E. Putnam, New York, 1852, p.79.

3   John Hopkins Medicine, 'Health Library: Risks of Physical Inactivity' John Hopkins Medicine, https://www.hopkinsmedicine.org/healthlibrary/conditions/cardiovascular_diseases/risks_of_physical_inactivity_85,p00218, (accessed 5 November 2019).

4   World Health Organization, 'Physical Inactivity: A Global Public Health Problem', https://www.who.int/dietphysicalactivity/factsheet_inactivity/en/), 2008, (accessed 2 September 2019).

5   Andrea F. Taylor & Frances E. Kuo, 'Children with attention deficits concentrate better after walk in the park', *Journal of Attention Disorders,* Vol. 12, 2009, p. 402.

6   Omid Kardan, Peter Gozdyra, Bratislav Misic, Faisal Moola, Lyle J. Palmer, Tomáš Paus & Marc G. Berman, 'Neighborhood greenspace and health in a large urban center', *Nature, Scientific Reports*, Vol. 5, article 11610, 2015, doi:10.1038/srep11610

7   Jenna H. Tilt, Thomas M. Unfried & Belén C. Roca, 'Using Objective and Subjective Measures of Neighborhood Greenness and Accessible Destinations for Understanding Walking Trips and BMI in Seattle, Washington', *American Journal of Health Promotion* Vol. 21, issue 4, 2007, pp. 371–379.

8   Peter Harnik Ben Welle, 'Measuring the Economic Value of a City Park System', The Trust for Public Land, Washington, DC, 2009.

9   Ioan Voicu Vicki Been, 'The effect of community gardens on neighboring property values', *Real Estate Economics,* Vol. 36, issue 2, 2008, pp. 241–283.

10   Judith H. Heerwagen, 'Investing in People: The Social Benefits of Sustainable Design', *Presented at Rethinking Sustainable Construction,* Sarasota, FL, 2006.

11   Frances E. Kuo & William C. Sullivan, 'Aggression and Violence in the Inner City: Effects of Environment via Mental Fatigue', *Environment and Behavior,* Vol. 33, issue 4, 2001, pp. 543–571.

12   Frances E. Kuo & William C. Sullivan, 'Environment and Crime in the Inner City: Does Vegetation Reduce Crime?', *Environment and Behavior,* Vol. 33, issue 3, 2001, pp. 343–367.

13   Adam Ganser, 'High Line Magazine: B1G DA+A and Parks', *Friends of the High Line*, https://www.thehighline.org/blog/2017/01/18/high-line-magazine-b1g-daa-and-parks/, 2017, (accessed 2 November 2019).

14   Michael Levere, 'The High Line park and timing of capitalization of public goods', *Department of Economics, University of California San Diego*, http://docplayer.net/42473681-The-high-line-park-and-timing-of-capitalization-of-public-goods.html, 2014, (accessed 14 September 2019).

15   Joseph Clancy & Cory Nestor, 'Paley Park, Urban Refuge', *Terrapin Bright Green*, https://www.terrapinbrightgreen.com/wp-content/uploads/2015/11/Paley-Park_Case-Study-Fall-15.pdf, 2015, (accessed 2 August 2019).

TOOLKIT

1   Rachel Kaplan, Stephen Kaplan & Robert L. Ryan, *With People in Mind, Design and Management of Everyday Nature*, Island Press, 1998.

GLOSSARY OF TERMS

1   James J. Gibson, *The Ecological Approach to Visual Perception*, Houghton Mifflin Harcourt (HMH), Boston, 1979.

2   Zakaria Djebbara, Lars Brorson Fich, Laura Petrini & Klaus Gramann, 'Sensorimotor brain dynamics reflect architectural affordances', *PNAS* July 16, 2019, 116 (29) pp. 14769–14778.

3   Michel Cabanac, 'Pleasure: the common currency', *Journal of Theoretical Biology*, 1992 Mar 21, 155(2), pp. 173–200. See also, Richard de Dear, 'Revisiting an Old Hypothesis of Human Thermal Perception: Alliesthesia', *Building Research & Information*, 39, 2, 2011.

4   Joyce Kim, Stefano Schiavon & Gail Brager, 'Personal comfort models – A new paradigm in thermal comfort for occupant-centric environmental control', *Building and Environment*, 2018, Vol. 132, pp. 114–124, and Thomas Parkinson, Richard de Dear, & Christhina Candido, 'Perception of Transient Thermal Environments: Pleasure and Alliesthesia', In Proceedings of 7th Windsor Conference, Windsor, UK, 2012.

5   Stephen Kaplan, 'The restorative benefits of nature: Toward an integrative framework', *Journal of Environmental Psychology*, September 1995, Vol 15, issue 3, pp. 169–182.

6   Lee, K. Williams, L. Sargent, N. Williams & K. Johnson, '40-second green roof views sustain attention: The role of micro-breaks in attention restoration', *Journal of Environmental Psychology*, Volume 42, June 2015, pp. 182–189.

7   Erich Fromm, *The Heart of Man,* Harper & Row, 1964.

8   Erich Fromm, *The Anatomy of Human Destructiveness*, New York, Holt, Rinehart & Winston, 1973, pp. 365–366.

9   Edward O. Wilson, *Biophilia*, Harvard University Press, Cambridge, MA, 1984, p. 1.

10   Edward O. Wilson in Stephen R. Kellert & Edward O. Wilson (eds), *Biophilia Hypothesis*, Island Press, 1993, p. 31.

11   Stephen R. Kellert, 'Introduction', in Stephen R. Kellert & Edward O. Wilson, *Biophilia Hypothesis*, Island Press, 1993, p. 21.

12   Stephen R. Kellert & Elizabeth F. Calabrese 'The practice of biophilic design', http://www.biophilic-design.com, 2015, pp. 6–7 (accessed 20 August 2019).

13   Marco Casagrande, 'From Urban Acupuncture to the Third Generation City', *Journal of Biourbanism*, Vol. 4, 2016, pp. 29–42.

14   Nikos A. Salingaros & Kenneth G. Masden II, 'Intelligence-Based Design: A Sustainable Foundation for Worldwide Architectural Education', *Archnet International Journal of Architectural Research,* 2008,Vol. 2, issue 1, pp. 129–188. See also, Orr, op. cit., pp. 415–421.

15   Joan I. Nassauer, 'Messy Ecosystems, Orderly Frames', *Landscape Journal,* 1995, 14 (2), pp. 161–169.

16   John D. Balling & John H. Falk, 'Development of Visual Preference for Natural Environments', *Environment and Behavior,* 1982, Vol. 14, issue 1, pp. 5–28.

17   Ann Forsyth & Laura R. Musacchio, *Designing Small Parks: A Manual for Addressing Social and Ecological Concerns,* John Wiley & Sons, Inc., New Jersey, 2005, pp. 13–30, 60–65, 74–82, 95–98.

18   Salingaros & Masden, loc. cit.

19   Daniel Pauly, 'Anecdotes and the shifting baseline syndrome of fisheries'. *Trends in Ecology and Evolution*, 1995, Vol. 10, issue 10, p. 430.

20   Peter H. Kahn, Jr., Rachel L. Severson & Jolina H. Ruckert, 'The Human Relation with Nature and Technological Nature', *Current Directions in Psychological Science,* 2009, Vol. 18, issue 1, pp. 37–42.

21   Richard Louv, *Last Child in the Woods: Saving Our Children from Nature-Deficit Disorder,* Workman Publishing Company, 2005.

22   Nature and the Brain, National Geographic Society Innovation Grant, https://neurobiophilia.org/what-is-neurobiophilia/

23   Annemarie S. Dosen & Michael J. Ostwald, 'Prospect and refuge theory: Constructing a critical definition for architecture and design', *International Journal of Design in Society,* 2013, Vol. 6, pp. 9–23.

24   William D. Browning & Dakota Walker, 'An Ear for Nature: Psychoacoustic strategies for workplace distraction and the bottom line', Terrapin Bright Green, LLC, New York, 2018.

25   Gregory N. Bratman, Christopher B. Anderson, Marc G. Berman, Bobby Cochran, Sjerp de Vries, Jon Flanders, Carl Folke, Howard Frumkin, James J. Gross, Terry Hartig, Peter H. Kahn Jr., Ming Kuo, Joshua J. Lawler, Phillip S. Levin, Therese Lindahl, Andreas Meyer-Lindenberg, Richard Mitchell, Zhiyun Ouyang, Jenny Roe, Lynn Scarlett, Jeffrey R. Smith, Matilda van den Bosch, Benedict W. Wheeler, Mathew P. White, Hua Zheng and Gretchen C. Daily, 'Nature and mental health: An ecosystem service perspective', *Science Advances:* Vol. 5, issue 7, 2019, DOI: 10.1126/sciadv.aax0903

26   https://living-future.org/declare/declare-about/red-list/

27   Yi-Fu Tuan, *Topophilia: A Study of Environmental Perceptions, Attitudes, and Values*, Columbia University Press, 1990.

28   David R. Orr, 'Love It or Lose It: The Coming Biophilia Revolution,' in Stephen R. Kellert and Edward O. Wilson, editors, *The Biophilia Hypothesis*, Island Press, Washington DC, 1993, p. 422.

INDEX

IMAGE CREDITS